ATTU BOY

Nick Golodoff in Atka. *Brenda Maly*

ATTU BOY

A YOUNG ALASKAN'S WWII MEMOIR

Nick Golodoff

UNIVERSITY OF ALASKA PRESS | FAIRBANKS

University of Alaska Press
P.O. Box 756240
Fairbanks, AK 99775-6240

Library of Congress Cataloging-in-Publication Data

Maly, Brenda.
 Attu boy / Brenda Maly, Nick Golodoff & Rachel Mason.
   pages cm
 Includes bibliographical references and index.
 ISBN 978-1-60223-249-5 (pbk. : alk. paper) — ISBN 978-1-60223-250-1 (elecronic)
 1. Golodoff, Nick, 1935- 2. Attu Island (Alaska)--Biography. 3. Attu, Battle of, Alaska, 1943--Personal
narratives, American. 4. Prisoners of war--United States. 5. Prisoners of war--Japan--Shiritsu Otaru
Bungakkan. 6. Attu Island (Alaska)--History. 7. Attu Island (Alaska)--Social life and customs. 8.
World War, 1939-1945--Alaska--Aleutian Islands. I. Golodoff, Nick. II. Mason, Rachel, 1954- III.
Title.
 D769.87.A4M28 2015
 940.54>7252092--dc23
                            2014023205

Cover photo of Attu in 1938, Christine M. McClain Collection, UAA
Cover and interior design by Dixon Jones, Rasmuson Library Graphics

This publication was printed on acid-free paper that meets the minimum requirements for ANSI /
NISO Z39.48–1992 (R2002) (Permanence of Paper for Printed Library Materials).

An earlier edition of this book was published in 2012 by the National Park Service, US Department
of Interior, Aleutian World War II National Historic Area, Anchorage, Alaska. The project was
funded by the National Park Service, Affiliated Areas program in cooperation with the Aleutian
Pribilof Heritage Group.

CONTENTS

LIST OF FIGURES

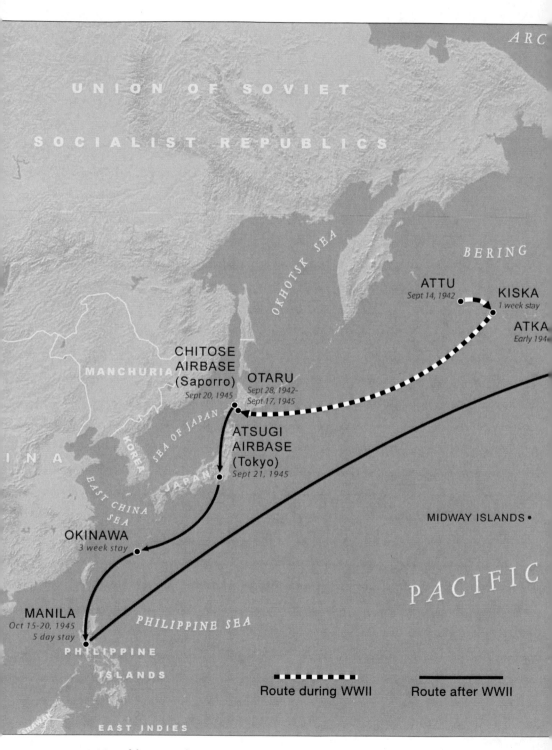

FIG. 1. Map of the Attuans' Journey. *Adapted from National Park Service 2010. Projection WGS 1984 Web Mercator Auxiliary Sphere. Base image from World Shaded Relief Map compiled by ESRI ArcGIS Online and data partners*

ALASKA

EKLUTNA

ANCHORAGE

CANADA

GULF OF
ALASKA

DUTCH HARBOR,
UNALASKA

SEATTLE
Nov 20, 1945
1 month stay

TACOMA

UNITED

STATES

SAN FRANCISCO
Nov 3, 1945
1 week stay

OCEAN

MEXICO

HAWAII

Miles
0   400   800   1,600

Kilometers
0   500   1,000   2,000

PREFACE, 2012

Brenda Maly

NICK GOLODOFF'S GRANDDAUGHTER AND DESCENDANT OF ATTU

When you meet someone who has been through World War II and they tell you their amazing stories of what they went through or what they saw, from the listener's point of view it's very exciting to hear. But what if you put yourself in their place? Imagine what is going through your mind, your feelings, your wonderment, your losses, the unknown of what is going to happen, and the waiting. This can be a scary thought, especially if the stories are from someone you love dearly. Life does work out in mysterious ways, and you can't help but go with it. An early life experience can change your future in bad ways, but also in good ways. What I'm trying to say here is that life is unexpected, and back during World War II it was harsher than it is now. It had to be, or we would not be where we are now. My grandfather, Nick L. Golodoff, had no choice. He was taken off his island of Attu, Alaska, by the Japanese when he was very young. He witnessed an amazing event, World War II, from another view than most people. A lot of people talk about World War II from the United States' view. He tells the story of actually being captured by the Japanese. When you read this book, please keep in mind that Nick was about five or six years old when taken off Attu Island. Names and dates are blurry to him, and some things are uncertain. With Rachel Mason, our editor and good friend, and with our family, Nick and I have done our best to get any facts about World War II that are related to Nick's story. Most of the information needed is from Japan, and some information they would not release to us. My grandfather Nick wishes to be done with this book as soon as possible. This is his last and final wish before passing. This book is written from his point of view as a child and as he tells it, with some minor adjustments. A book with detailed facts and information from other sources takes some time, and Nick is elderly and just wishes to get his story out now rather than later. Please understand that this book is not perfection but his honest experience. It is a story that is most interesting.

Editor's note: This preface was written in 2012 for the National Park Service's publication of Attu Boy. *Nick Golodoff died on February 8, 2013.*

INTRODUCTION
Telling the Story of Attu

Rachel Mason

EDITOR

When Nick Golodoff was six years old, he and his family were taken from Attu, Alaska, to Japan, where they were held captive until the end of World War II. Nick has recorded and written his memories. His granddaughter Brenda Maly transcribed and compiled them, and they are intertwined here with several other firsthand accounts of the Attuan experience.

I learned of Nick Golodoff 's memoir in 2008 while working on the Lost Villages of the Aleutians project of the Aleutian World War II National Historic Area, National Park Service. The project documents the history of four Unangan villages left empty in the evacuations and relocations of World War II and never permanently resettled after the war. The residents of three villages in the Unalaska Island area (Biorka, Makushin, and Kashega) were removed to southeast Alaska in 1942 and were resettled in other Unangan villages upon their return in 1945. Attu had a different and more tragic story. In September 1942, the Japanese army took the forty-two Attu residents to Otaru, on Hokkaido Island, where they stayed until war's end. Many of them died, mainly of starvation and malnutrition. The twenty-five surviving Attuans were not able to return to their former village. Those who were not hospitalized (or sent to boarding school, as were several young people) were resettled in Atka.

In 2008, the Lost Villages project had already collected considerable material on the Unalaska Island area villages, thanks to a series of oral history interviews Ray Hudson collected in 2004. However, we had no firsthand information about Attu. At a meeting of the project's steering committee in Anchorage, I learned from Crystal Dushkin that Nick Golodoff had been working on a memoir entitled *Attu Boy*, about his experiences as a young boy at the time of the Japanese invasion, during the internment in Japan, through the Attuans' release and return to America, and finally to his life in Atka after he moved there at the age of nine. Crystal knew that Nick was looking for a publisher, but she did not know the status of his manuscript. She suggested that the National Park Service might be able to work out an agreement with Nick to publish his memoir as part of the Lost Villages project.

Starting in 2004, Nick began recording and writing his memories at his home in Atka. This account originated in tapes Nick made and sent to his granddaughter Brenda Maly in Anchorage. Over the next few years, Brenda transcribed and edited the accounts. When I began work on the project, I rearranged Nick's statements in chronological order. I researched other accounts and found several other first-hand narratives of the Attuans' experience. Besides Nick Golodoff, these include Innokenty Golodoff (Nick's father's brother), Olean Golodoff Prokopeuff (Nick's mother), Mike Lokanin, and Alex Prossoff.

Innokenty Golodoff, Nick's father's half-brother, was born in 1917 on Attu to Metrofan and Anastasia Golodoff. Anastasia was Metrofan's second wife. Innokenty was known throughout his life as Popeye. After the Attuans were settled in Atka, Popeye married Vasha Nevzoroff there in 1947. They had two daughters and a son. Popeye died in Anchorage in 1998.

Olean Golodoff Prokopeuff, Nick's mother, was born Olean Horosoff in 1910 in Atka to Peter and Anna Horoshoff. She married Lovrenti Golodoff and moved to Attu, where they had seven children, all of whom were taken to Japan. Lovrenti and three of their children died in Japan. Nick's older brother John survived, as did his younger siblings Gregory and Elizabeth. Olean and her children were resettled in Atka after the war, and in 1947 she married Ralph Prokopeuff. They had three children. Olean died in Anchorage in about 1976.

Mike or Mihie Lokanin (sometimes written Lukanin) was born in 1912, either in Attu or Unalaska, to Ephem and Anna Lukanin. His mother was from Makushin. Mike's first marriage, to Mary Tarkanoff, ended in divorce in 1939. In 1940 Mike married Parascovia Horosoff, Olean Golodoff's younger half-sister, on Attu. Their first three children died, two of them in Japan. Parascovia had six more children before Mike died in Unalaska in 1961.

Alex Prossoff was born in 1916 on Attu. His parents were Mike Prossoff and his first wife, Marina. Alex married Elizabeth Prokopeuff aboard the Coast Guard cutter *Itasca* in 1939. Elizabeth already had a daughter, Fekla, who took her step-father Alex's name. Alex died before 1949.

The first-person accounts of wartime events are quite different in style and form. Innokenty Golodoff's story was published in the *Alaska Sportsman* in December

Name	Age in June 1942	Year of Birth	Year of Death
Nick Golodoff	6	1935	2013
Innokenty "Popeye" Golodoff	25	1917	1998
Olean Golodoff Prokopeuff	31	1911	ca. 1976
Mike Lokanin	30	1912	1961
Alex Prossoff	29	1916	Before 1949

FIG. 2. Table of five personal narratives of the Attuans' experience in Japan

1966, "as told to" Kent W. Kenyon, a biologist for the US Fish and Wildlife Service. Olean Golodoff Prokopeuff was interviewed by Knut Bergsland, and her account appeared in the Aleutian-Pribilof Island Association newsletter. The translation was later revised by Moses Dirks and published in *The Aleutian Invasion*, a project of high school students in Unalaska (Unalaska City Schools 1981). In 1946 or 1947 Mike Lokanin and Alex Prossoff wrote their own stories, which were published verbatim in Ethel Ross Oliver's *Journal of an Aleutian Year* (1988). In this 2015 edition of *Attu Boy*, Mike Lokanin's written account has been edited for readability.

Following common usage in America during World War II, the Attuans who told of their experience referred to the Japanese as "Japs." The word has been retained in the first-person accounts. It is notable, however, that unlike other Attuans who remembered being held prisoner in Japan, Nick Golodoff never used this term in his recollections of Japanese people.

Much of the Attuans' experience in Japan has remained obscure, partly because few of the survivors were inclined to talk about their experiences there. There is not much of a written record either. They did not keep diaries or write letters from Japan. In addition, participants in the wartime events have divergent memories of what happened. Perhaps especially because they have not discussed their experiences with one another, there are multiple accounts of these traumatic events.

To provide a context to the firsthand accounts, I added background material, culled from published and unpublished sources, about Attu history, prehistory, and the events of World War II. Nick Golodoff's is the most complete account yet of the years in Japan, from the unique perspective of a young boy. His book is a gift not only to the descendants of Attu and to other Unangan but to all of us who need to hear this previously untold story. Thank you to all those who helped assemble this memoir. I would like particularly to thank Shannon Apgar-Kurtz, Anna Bateman, Francis Broderick (designer), Omar Chavez, Janet Clemens, John

Cloe, Linda Cook, Debbie Corbett, Crystal Dushkin, Nicole Ferreira (cartographer), Ray Hudson, Janis Kozlowski, Bruce Greenwood, Jennifer Jolis, and Dirk Spennemann.

A YOUNG BOY'S EXPERIENCE DURING WORLD WAR II

There are many books about the Aleutian Islands in Alaska during World War II, but hardly any books about the invasion of Attu Island and the personal experiences of those who lived through it. In most books that I have read about World War II in the Aleutian Islands, there is some truth, but there is a lot of dishonesty in the books. I know this because I have been through it. I am also talking about Aleuts in this book because I never saw any true stories about Aleuts. Not all the books that I have read and seen are all true. Some books I have read about Aleuts in this region from Attu to Atka contain false information. I'm talking about my own experiences so people will know what happened to me. I also want to sell my book in Japan. Some people there are interested in what I did during and after the war.

The stories in this book are personal to me, as are the feelings I have felt through this unexpected, frightening, and life-altering ordeal. I have told these stories to many individuals and in their expressions and questions, they were perplexed by what I have gone through. After telling my stories I was asked if I was going to write a book about my life, and so here it is. Please, know that I am going to be seventy-six years old by the end of 2011 and I don't remember everything about my childhood, but I do remember well my experience during World War II.

I was born December 19, 1935, about thirty miles southwest of Attu during trapping season. It was winter and my parents were fox trapping on Agattu Island. Dad made most of the family's living from trapping. Before the war they used to trap on all the islands. They trapped white, gray, silver, and blue fox. The trappers took their furs to the store and traded them for things like flour, sugar, and other food. There was a boat that used to come from Seattle to collect the furs. Before people trapped for fox, they used to hunt sea otters and fur seals for the furs. There was no trapping during the war.

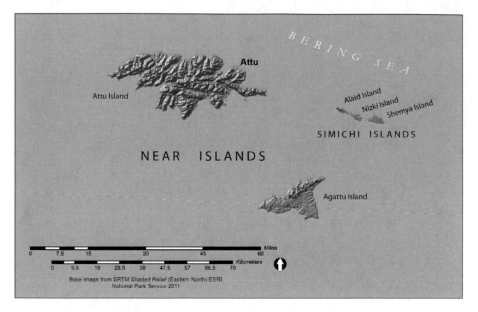

FIG. 3. Map of the Near Islands

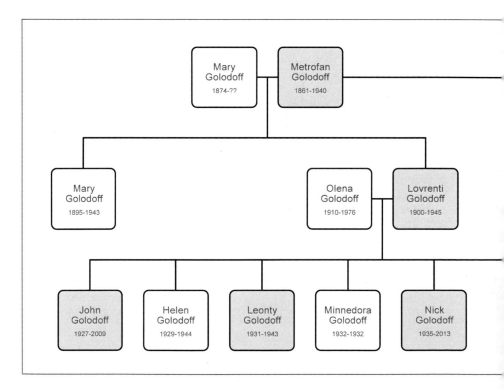

FIG. 4. Nick's family in 1942. *Adapted from Family Echo www.familyecho.com*

While they were trapping they lived in a mud house, like a barabara. My dad's name was Lovrenti Golodoff. My mom's name was Olena Horisoff.[1] She was from Atka, and my parents met in Atka. My father's brother Innokenty was with them on Agattu Island when I was born. Aleuts have Russian names because the Russians gave the Aleuts family names and new names when they baptized the Aleuts.

My uncle told me that when I was a baby, he used to let me suck on a sea urchin. At that time babies didn't have any milk other than from their mom. We would pick up sea urchins at low tide. We ate seaweed too.

After the winter I was born, neither my mother nor I ever went back to Agattu after that. I lived on Attu until I was a little over six years old. When the Japanese invaded the island of Attu, I was taken as a prisoner of war to Japan. I was in Japan for more than three years. On the way back from Japan to Atka, we stopped at a few places like Okinawa, Manila, San Francisco, Seattle, Adak, and then Atka. I have been living here in Atka ever since. As an adult I did go back once to work on Attu, but I didn't see the village again.

---

[1] In lists of Attu residents, Nick's father's name is usually spelled "Lavrenti" and his mother's "Olean."

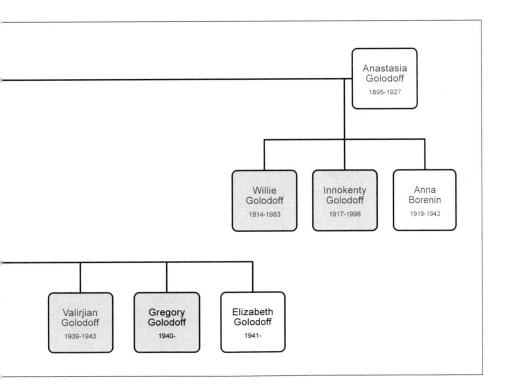

Attu in 1938, mislabeled as "Kiska."

Christine M. McClain Collection, Archives and Special Collections, Consortium Library, University of Alaska Anchorage

"Wide view of village and harbor," taken before World War II.

Alaska State Library, Dora M. Sweeney Collection

The "Main Street" of Attu. Nick's house is the one with two men standing in front of it. *Alan G. May papers, Archives and Special Collections, Consortium Library, University of Alaska Anchorage*

Attu before the War

In 1942 before the war began, Attu was a nice, quiet place with a population of about thirty-four people.[2] We had nothing: no insulation in the houses and no inside plumbing. There was a wood stove to heat the house. Attu was plain and quiet all the time. There was a trading post, church, and some houses. Some people were still living in barabaras. The BIA school had a white teacher and her husband. People did not have much to do since there were hardly any jobs. The only source of money was trapping during the winter, and during the summer they just dried, salted, or smoked salmon and did some woodcarving. I was only six years old during this time, so I did not have much to do besides walking the pathways. There were only a few of them, and they were nothing but gravel. One went from one end of the village to the other end and the other went down to the beach. The main one was from the church to the school. There were no streets, just paths. Back then everyone in the village used to help or work voluntarily, but today people work only if you pay them.

I have a picture of my house in Attu with my dad standing outside with someone (above). I remember the inside of the house. It had two rooms; one room had beds,

---

[2]   The 1940 US Census shows forty-four residents in Attu village.

Children playing outside their home.
Alan G. May papers, Archives and Special Collections, Consortium Library, University of Alaska Anchorage

and the other had a table and a stove, and also we had an attic, which we used for storage. I remember while I was in Attu, one morning in winter when I got up, my house was dark so I thought it was still night. My dad went out and made steps out of snow to the top of the almost-built house and after I went outside I could only see chimneys and the smoke coming out where the house should be. I remember the house used to be cold in the morning because we only had a wood stove and the house was not insulated. I know where my house was because it was the second from the other end, on the school side. I used to know the man who lived next door, but cannot remember the name.

Attu is just like any other Aleutian island. It has more gravel than any other Aleutian island I have been on, too, and it has rougher country. There is very little sand. I don't remember any volcanoes on the island. Attu does have bushes that Atka doesn't have.

I used to like going out in the boat and still do. I could not live without the sight of the ocean, so when the weather was nice I would be at the beach almost every day. Whenever I needed wood or to go hunting, I was at the beach wanting to go out in the boat, but the adults would not take me, and if they did not I was told I would cry and throw rocks at them.

Sometimes after church, my parents used to tell me to get my godfather and bring him over to our house for tea. I was told to not let him walk in the puddles

View of Attu showing several homes, and a wooden plank pathway in the foreground.
Alan G. May papers, Archives and Special Collections, Consortium Library, University of Alaska Anchorage

because he was blind. I guess I was a bad boy because I used to let him walk in the puddles and he never said anything till he got to my house. Then he would tell my parents what I did. I would get kicked out of the house, but I would still do it.

Prewar Fears and Clues about Japanese Invasion

Before the war, some trappers from the village didn't return. They found them shot on Attu. The old-timers thought it was the Japanese who shot them. When the Attuan men would go hunting on Attu, they used to see other people. Later they learned that the Japanese were mapping in the area.

Before the Japanese came to Attu, a man used to talk about seeing tracks when he had to go walking. He would see tracks on the beach and sometimes he would see somebody and when he hollered to that person, it would disappear. I figure now they were Japanese mapping the island before they invaded it. The same thing happened on Atka and Unalaska. They used to call them *"Tuginagus,"* which means boogieman.[3] When a man from Attu went and checked his traps, he returned and asked the people in the village who was out hunting earlier. He was told that no

---

3   Bergsland (1980:43, 142) says *chugdukaayax^* means "Devil" and *tugidax^* means "moon" in Atkan Unangam Tunuu. In the dialect of the Eastern Aleutians, also according to Bergsland (1994:99), an "outside man, outlaw, fugitive" is called *asx^ aadax^* . The word in the Attu dialect is not included in the dictionary.

one left the village besides him. Therefore, no one knew and no one understood what was going on. Just before the war started, I also saw a man, a ghost and his son. The elders, they told me stories of what might have happened. We thought the man killed his son then himself but there were no rifles nearby, so we guessed it was the Japanese while they were mapping the area from Attu to Unalaska. The reason I am saying this is because after the war, people went trapping again but never found tracks or saw ghosts anymore.

I think the Japanese were all over the Aleutians before the war because after the war, the elders were talking about seeing people when everybody was in the village and seeing mysterious tracks, not just on one island but all the other islands. People also heard boat engines. After the war, no one talked about boogiemen anymore.

The Japanese Invasion, June 7, 1942

The Attuans had been warned by the US military that the Japanese might come. Before the US could evacuate the Attuans, the Japanese invaded. The teacher, Etta Jones, told them about Pearl Harbor. Her husband had a radio.

When the Japanese arrived, it was a nice calm day. Now I know that it was June 7, 1942, but I didn't know it then. The whole village of Attu was in church that Sunday morning. As I was going to church, I looked up and saw Jesus coming down real slow. I turned around to see if anyone else was looking, and when I turned back he was gone.

Once church was over, we all heard noises that sounded like motors from the next bay. It was a sound we had never heard and turned out to be machine gun fire. Four or five young men were sent up a hill to look. By the time they figured out what the noise was it was too late; the Japanese were already there. Then we saw a plane go over the village. This plane flew over once. The plane had a red round symbol on the wing, and the plane was so close to the ground we could see the pilot.

When I saw Alex Prossoff heading down to the beach, I started to follow him thinking he was going boating and that I could come along. Just before I caught up with Alex, on the way down, there was a platform where they were going to build a house. On the platform there was a gunnysack spread over it. While Alex and I were down at the beach, we heard sounds and voices that we did not understand. The Japanese were loud as they came down the side of the mountain. We heard a noise that sounded like crows. Every time I looked I didn't see anything. We started to hear shooting, so Alex ran and I followed. Alex and I ran past the church to the other side of the village and that's where we saw the Japanese soldiers coming down the hill. While I was still running after Alex, I could see a piece of mud popping up in front of me, so I stopped. I looked back, and the mud behind me was popping up. The reason we were not hit is that the bullets did not reach us, but they came only one or two feet short of the path we were running on. I did not understand the mud popping up at the time, but now I understand that the Japanese were shooting at us. Alex and I were lucky to get away.

Alex was still running, so I continued following him. When Alex reached his house, he went under it. His wife was already hiding under their house, so Alex crawled in. When I tried to go under I was told to go in the mud house,[4] which was behind the house Alex was under, and that is what I did. They had a barabara behind Alex's house that was his old house before they built a wooden one. It was used for storage. Someone opened the door to the mud house for me.

When the Japanese landed in Attu, I wonder why they were shooting when they were coming down the hill. I think because everybody was outside listening to the noise from the next harbor where they were landing and nobody knew what was going on. The reason the Attu people were all outside was that there was all kinds of noise from the next bay to the village. That is my first time I have seen so many people out at the same time.

When we went up, we saw a Japanese plane go over, and then later the Japanese came down the hill shooting. The school teacher's husband had a radio, but they did not send out a message until the Japanese were almost to the school. Then they started to send a message, and the Japanese took over the school and cut them off. During the gunfire, I believe the Japanese killed their own people because I heard that one or two of the Japanese people were dead. The only person that was hit from Attu was one woman who was shot in the leg.

While I was in the mud house, I heard people outside speaking a different language. It was lucky that Alex went under the house because if he wasn't there, the Japanese would have shot the mud house and could have killed us all. After the Japanese caught Alex and his wife under the house, they gave him a note. The note said that everyone had to come out, and if no one listened, the Japanese were going to blow up the house and mud house with machine guns. Alex translated what the Japanese wrote in English. If they told us to get out, we would not be able to understand, and the reason for the note, Alex told us, was that the Japanese know how to write in English but did not know how to speak it. Alex translated back to the Japanese in English.

We all went out, and the Japanese marched us all over to the school. That's where I met up with my mom and dad. I threw up when I got there because I was scared. I do not know how they got the other Attu people, but when we got to the school,

---

4   Nick uses the term "mud house" for the traditional Unangan semisubterranean dwelling commonly referred to as a barabara.

everybody was there except for the four men [teenagers] that went up the hill. Later they took two men from the village and a Japanese soldier to go up and look for them, and they hollered at them to come out to let them know everything was okay, and they brought them back. There was a teacher and wife [sic] in Attu, but I don't know what happened to them. The white couple were married, and Mrs. Jones was the teacher. I heard they both tried to kill themselves on Attu. I don't know what happened to them. They didn't want to be POWs, I guess. They cut their wrists only someone found out.[5]

I'm unsure how long they kept us there in the school, but it seemed like almost all day. Later that day, toward evening, the Japanese sent us all to our houses. Once we had gotten to our houses, the Japanese posted guards with guns at every house. The guard by our house didn't have any matches or a lighter, so he would knock on our door and ask for a match in Russian. My dad would give him matches. Our guard was nice—just like most Japanese people I know.

The next day I went out and walked around a bit. I cannot really recall what happened, but again, I was only six years old. Every day I would go out and walk around. I got familiar with the Japanese troops and they were friendly to me. When I would go down to the beach, there was a guard that had a box and inside it there was some candy. Every time that I saw him down at the beach, he'd offer me some. Behind each house, there was a mud house [barabara] and I believe that the Japanese troops were taking turns sleeping in them. I noticed behind the village there was a long mud house and I think they used it for cooking and a mess hall. The Japanese had foxholes all over Attu. One time I went to church and there were Japanese navy men living inside the church. They had beds on each side of the church. I am unsure why they cut the cross that was on top of the church. They used cloth as a net to catch trout with.

The Japanese commander used to take baths in drums. The Japanese soldier would put water in the drum and build a fire underneath it to heat the water and when the fire went out, he would take a bath. When Japanese purchased anything in Attu, they did not use money; they used fox fur. They would take their foxes to the store and were told how much it would cost and used furs to cover the purchase.

Early one morning while the Japanese occupied Attu, an American plane flew low over the village before anybody got up. Just before the American plane showed up, we heard a cannon go off at the point of the bay. That happened twice. I figured they were just taking pictures. The first time it happened, my mom and dad hid under the bed, but I was at the window. I saw a Japanese soldier come out in his

---

[5]   As discussed in the commentary on p. 50, although Japanese sources say Mr. Jones committed suicide, inhumation records show that he was shot in the head.

Alex and Elizabeth Prossoff. Nick hid under their barabara ("mud house") with them during the Japanese invasion. *Aleutian-Pribilof Island Association*

underwear running to a foxhole with his rifle. While this was going on, my dad grabbed me and pulled me under the bed with him. The second time the American plane flew over, my mom and dad went under the bed, and I ran to the window again. This time the Japanese soldier had his clothes on as he was running to the foxhole with his rifle.

Life as a Japanese POW

I guessed that the Japanese were planning to stay a while because they brought in extra supplies like onions and potatoes. Once the Japanese finished unloading supplies, I guess plans changed because they were leaving and they took us with them. At that time [mid-September], I did not understand why they did not leave us in Attu. While we were heading down to the beach, the Japanese were burning the onions and potatoes. My mom gave me some cooked potatoes off the beach so I had some. The Japanese took us out to the boat and put us in the cargo hold, where we stayed all the way to Tokyo. They dropped off some Japanese troops

Attu schoolhouse. *UAF Historical Photograph Collection, Vertical File Photograph Collections-Towns-Attu*

Etta Jones and Foster Jones. "Sad fate of Attu's only white couple."
UAF, San Francisco Call-Bulletin, Aleutian Islands Photographs, 1942–1948

there. From Tokyo we went to the island of Hokkaido, which is where we were held until the war was over. We were taken to Sapporo, the largest city on Hokkaido.[6]

The next thing I knew, we were in a house and we weren't allowed to leave. In Japan, they put us all in one building for over three years with one Japanese police officer guarding us. The building we were kept in was made out of wood; there were two levels, and I stayed on the second floor. There were two planks under a building for a bathroom. Coal was piled under the house. There wasn't a sink. I remember my mom used to wipe my hands with a wet cloth. The house must have had a stove to provide heat, but I don't remember it.

When we first got there, we used to eat only rice, oats, and fish, but later as the war was still going on there was hardly any food. Even the Japanese did not have much food.

I did not know what the men did for work, but I know that my mom worked digging the clay and I would go with her to work. There were two or three Japanese women working with Mom. I do not know how long they worked during the day, but we used to walk there and walk back home. I used to walk with my mom to and from the clay pits. Other than that, I never left that building.

At the first house, I had to stay inside most of the time. It felt like time was going slow since there was not much to do. I spent most of my time looking out the window.

Sometime during the war, I was taken to another building. During the last year of the war, I was able to go out. The Attuans were able to go out and find food for themselves. The second building was bigger and had a fence around it. There was a sour green apple tree and peach or apricot tree nearby. The policeman wouldn't let us climb the trees. During the summer, the fruit started dropping. Early in the morning, I used to get up, pick them off the ground, and eat some. Going out and doing things kept me going. I also spent a lot of time sitting inside by the window and watching the Japanese go by. In the morning, I could hear Japanese women with wooden shoes walking down the street, and it would wake me up. I didn't talk to the Japanese. A little boy would come to the fence to play with me, but I was too afraid to go outside the fence.

At the second building, there was a hospital above us where our people were taken when they were sick. I am unsure what kind of sickness they had, but most of them were in the hospital. Hardly anyone was in the building. My dad was in the hospital as well, and sometimes in the morning, my mom and I would walk upstairs to visit him and return in the evening. My dad died soon after we moved to

---

[6] The Attuans may have stopped in Sapporo, but they were taken to Otaru, another city on Hokkaido, for the duration of the war.

the second house. I was seven or eight when he died. When I was in Japan in 1992 [actually 1995] I asked for my dad's medical record, but they would not give it to me. I had an older sister, too, Helen. I don't know what happened to her—maybe she died in Japan. I didn't know about any of my siblings. I thought I was alone.

Many of the Attu people were sick. Many of the Attu people were dying. About half of them died. I am not sure exactly what happened, but they were dying one by one. When we were in the second building, I think during the last year we were there, just Steve Hodikoff and I were in the building, and everyone else was in the hospital. I was kind of surprised when Steve said to be quiet and a ghost came through the door. It walked in when we were both on the bed. The ghost walked in and turned around then went back out. We could see right through the ghost, but it was all white. The next day somebody else passed away.

The people who died were cremated and their ashes were put in pans. My dad got cremated, too. After the war ended their remains were shipped to Atka and buried.

I remember this one woman had a hole on top of her feet. This woman must have been related to me somehow because my mom would take me to her. Every time I went to visit, the hole on the top of her feet got bigger and bigger, and then she passed away. I myself had the same problem. The hole on top of my feet was getting bigger. I do not know what they did to it, but it started drying up and healed completely. I do not know what the cause of it was. Today I still have a scar from it.

I was told that when I was in Japan, I was in the hospital, too. I do not remember what happened exactly. I was taken there in a covered wagon with Japanese pulling me. It had two wheels and was all covered.[7] A Japanese man was pulling me to another building. When I got there, they put me in a room with a window and told me to stay in my room, and so I did. I didn't know why I was separated from my mom. I cannot remember how long I stayed. I used to get a quarter of a bowl of watery rice a day, and sometimes oats and water. I could see through the window, but all I could see was ground. I was rooming with a Japanese boy younger than I was, and his mom would come and visit him once in a while. I noticed that his mother did not like me very much. When the Japanese boy and his mother were talking, I could not understand what they were saying. After a while, I picked up a few things because I started to learn the Japanese language.

When I got back to my mom, I was told I was skin and bones. When I was in the hospital, I used to daydream about a big house by the beach, and pies, and cakes. Back when I was in Attu, I did not have many pies or cakes. In fact, I do not

---

[7] Perhaps this human-powered wheeled transportation was a rickshaw.

remember having a birthday party in my life. Even when I came back to the United States, I do not remember having a birthday party.

I remember being hungry. The Attuan boys would steal food at night. They stole carrots, potatoes, and turnips. The boys shared the food with everyone so no one would tell on them. There was no meat but there was a little bit of fish. I ate some seaweed.

I did not have shoes while I was in Japan. I do not know how or when I got them, but I had wooden slippers. Every morning on the pavement, you could hear wooden slippers clapping every morning, and that is what used to wake me up. Since there was a fence around our building, we were able to step out. Every time I got up, I went out the back door to get some fresh air.

I could see the train station from where I stayed, and I watched some military men training the station workers to be in the military. There was a one skinny, tall Japanese military man trainee, and this trainer kept slapping him very often, so I guessed he did not like this tall person.

We spoke Aleut among ourselves. While we were in Japan, a police officer and his wife lived with us for over three years. They communicated with us by writing in English. Most of the Japanese could write English, but they couldn't speak it. My mom knew how to read and write English. My parents spoke some Russian, and the languages got mixed.

We were told that America was losing the war. I do not know why they were telling us that, but that is what they wanted us to believe, I guess. We didn't have any TV or radio, but the policeman had a radio, so I could hear some Japanese music and someone talking over the radio. The police officer had his own room; I never was in that room, so I do not really know what it was, but from that music I started to learn to sing. I remembered all the songs, and I started learning the language, like "one, two, three, four, five" in Japanese. Just as I was learning, I left and started to forget. While in Japan I hardly talked much, since there were not many people to talk to. I just listened and learned from that.

I think it was during the last year of the war, at night I could hear projectiles exploding and see searchlights. American planes were flying high, and I could hear the Japanese shooting at them. I never got hurt while I was in Japan.

Close to the end of the war, my mom and the police officer's wife took me to a place that was like a small pool, and I enjoyed it very much. It was supposed to be for a bath. I wanted to play there but I was told to hurry up, so I did. I do not remember getting back to the place where I was staying.

One day toward the end of the three years in Japan, the policeman took us down to the beach, and we saw Japanese women diving for sea urchins. None of us knew how to dive or wanted to dive, and it was too cold, so we just watched. Later we started moving some big boulders around and found some small crabs and picked some. When we got home, we cooked some and ate them. They were really good. There was not much to eat but it helped. I don't remember how often we ate. Near the end we started getting some better food. I think maybe it was because the Japanese were losing and they didn't want the Attuans telling everyone we didn't get fed well. Late in the third year we started to get kite fish. One time a police officer took a couple of younger men and me to go shopping. There were a few kite fish, oats, and a little bit of rice for sale. The police officer tried to get some oats, but the store would not give us any since there was not enough. Once we got home, the Japanese cooked some food for us. Even when I was hungry, I did not eat much since I did not like the kite fish very much. The kite fish meat was like glue; it was sticky, and I did not want eat any more even though I was hungry.

Most Japanese were kind. One time there were a few Japanese police officers who came and visited us, and one officer was somewhat mean.

Return and Resettlement

As the end of the war approached, we were still in Japan. The policeman told us the war was over, and we painted POW on the outside of our building so the American planes would know where we were. The planes flew over and looked around and saw it, and then the next day they came back with drums filled with food, all kinds of food, and they dropped the drums from the plane with a parachute. Their aim was not very good. Some drums filled with food fell into one of the Japanese houses and the policeman had to go and collect them.

I do not know how they got drums up to our building, but we ate well that day. Everything tasted good to me. I really liked the canned peaches. It was the first time I saw American sugar. After that I do not remember much, but we were still there for at least a week or two before the Americans arrived and moved us out.

While we were in Japan, we did not know Americans dropped the atomic bomb on Japan. No one told us about it. We did not know this until we got back to the United States. The policeman was happy for us that we were leaving. I liked Japan, but I was glad not to be living there anymore.

After the Americans found us, they put us on a bus. We didn't know where we were going, but they took us to the airport. Then they put us on a military plane with aluminum bucket seats on each side with seat belts. From Hokkaido, we went to Okinawa. I don't remember how long we stayed in Okinawa. All I remember is that we sat by a long table with a lot of food and my stomach was shrunk so I couldn't eat much, but I was very satisfied. From Okinawa, I do not know how I got to Manila but I remember I was there with a bunch of military men. I slept in a big army tent with a man from Attu; we used to watch movies outside. I had my first Coca-Cola in Manila.

I do not know where my mom was while I was in Manila, but I was with a military man and an Aleut man from Attu, and I remember we used to go to the mess hall and eat. We lived in a tent, and I remember it was warm, and we had mosquito nets around our bed, and sometimes we rode around with a few military men. Sometimes when we rode, I used to see what looked like hippopotamuses in the muddy pools around Manila. One day I had my first ice cream, something sweet and cold that I never had before, and that is what made me sick. I vomited, and they took me to a hospital. While I was in the hospital, I looked out the window: it was blowing wind, and the army tents were blowing in the air. Wood and tin were flying all over, trucks were rolling over. It was windy that whole day. We were hungry, so one of the male nurses went to the kitchen to get some sandwiches. He put them into a packsaddle and crawled all the way to the mess hall and brought us some sandwiches. It was so windy he had to crawl. Later I heard about a man and woman that were inside the big heavy metal van, and the man from Attu was hiding behind the outside freezer. They had twelve big freezers outside and the man from Attu was hiding behind them. I was lucky I was in the hospital that time.

I do not really know what happened next, but after awhile we went on a big army transport ship with thousands of military soldiers, from Manila to San Francisco.[8] The soldiers didn't have guns, just bayonets. It took ten or eleven days, but it felt like it took forever to get from Manila to San Francisco because we were on the boat, and most of the time we were in our rooms. When we went to the galley to eat, there were no tables or chairs. We had to stand up at the counter and eat our meals, and then had to leave so the others could eat too. Every day they used to give us a piece of paper that showed where we were. I do not know how long it took, but we were told we were going to go under the San Francisco Golden Gate Bridge. When we were close to the Golden Gate Bridge, we went out on the deck and I was looking for it. The bridge was not golden but it was nice, sunny, and calm, and I looked at the tall buildings. When we got alongside the dock, the military got off the boat first. We had to wait for somebody to come pick us up in a bus.

When the government workers picked us up, they took us to a hotel where we stayed, but I do not know for how long. I remember eating with my mom and

---

[8] The Attuans sailed on the USNS *General A. W. Brewster*. It was a new boat, launched in January 1945. When the Japanese surrendered, the *Brewster* was in the Philippines. It carried returning troops, and the Attuans, to San Francisco, arriving on September 1, 1945 (Naval History Online 2011).

brothers and sister at the hotel restaurant. While we were in San Francisco, I stayed in a room with my mom. She was scared of something outside the window. It was windy and raining and something outside the window was knocking. My mom thought someone was outside the window, so she went down to the desk and told them, and the guy came out and looked out and said there was no one out there. From San Francisco, we took a train to Seattle. We had to sleep on the train, and I found out it was hard to walk on the train while moving. I am not sure how long it took to travel from San Francisco to Seattle by train.

In Seattle, we lived in a hotel at first, but I do not know how long we stayed in the hotel. Later we moved to a house. Just my mom and I were in a house by ourselves. These houses were lined up alongside of a road. There was hardly any traffic on that road. Staying here was nice. I am not sure how long we stayed, but it may have lasted about a month or so. When you walked down to the main road, there was a lot of traffic.

We were up on a hill. There was a bike shop close by and they were renting out bikes for fifty cents an hour. This is where I learned to ride a bike. I used to rent a bike almost every day and practice. I had scars and bruises all over from practicing to learn how to ride a bicycle, but I learned. My first time seeing a horse is when my older brother John rented a horse, and I was somewhat scared since it was a big horse. The weather in Seattle was nice practically every day. I used to watch one man hitting golf balls. He would hit the balls out in a field and leave them there; I am guessing he was practicing. Once he was done, I went out to the field and picked many golf balls up. Next day when we showed up, I gave them to him and he gave me fifty cents, so I went and rented a bike again. I am not sure where I got all my fifty cents from but my mom, I think, gave me fifty cents every day. I did not have much to do. I did not see any other kids, it was just me. Sometimes I was the only one in the neighborhood since it was so quiet. Sometimes people would knock on our door selling us turkey, chicken, and stuff like that. I remember my mom brought a turkey for around two dollars, and I do not remember us eating it.

The Attuans wanted to go back to Attu. Halfway back to the United States, we were told that we were going to Atka and not Attu. Mom told me we had relatives in Atka.

After Seattle, I do not know how we got to Adak. Once we got to Adak, there were nothing but military people there. Adak was cold and I didn't like it. I didn't know what I was getting into but I followed my mom. I do not know how long we stayed in Adak, but I remember coming to Atka on a small military barge. It was only about fifty feet square with a black bottom.

When we got to Atka, the Aleuts there were building houses with leftover

Nick's wife Vasha Golodoff and three of their children. *Nick Golodoff*

military lumber, so we had to stay with other families before they built us small houses to live in. My mom was from Atka, so we stayed with relatives. There was lots of material to build houses. After that they built us a bigger, better place to stay.

Atka was a lot like Attu. The bay looked the same and the hills and land almost similar, but at Attu there were bushes, and there were none here in Atka. When we arrived, the military men were still here in Atka. I did not see any planes, boats, big guns, or tanks, but they were still there, leaving slowly. Every six months some of the military people kept leaving until there were only five left. Then after that, they closed down Atka and all left. The military left behind a metal airstrip about three thousand feet long and lots of Quonset huts, a big plane hangar, cold storage, and a big wooden mess hall. They left them all and took off. There was some lumber left over, which we used to build houses, and then everything started rusting. What was left and useless, we used to burn. We did not have indoor plumbing, so we used to haul water from creeks. To take a bath, we used to heat water on top of the stove, and my family had no money so we had to live off the land, eating things like fish from the creek, roots, berries, sea urchins, mussels, clams, etc. But I still had better food than I ate when I was in Japan.

Cover of *Meetings between Aleutian and Japanese People* by Masami Sugiyama, published in Japan, 1987.

Nick's Connection to Japan

I call the author [Masami Sugiyama] "Sam." He came to Atka three or four times. He sent me that picture. The last time Sam came, they took me back to Japan.[9] I don't know the name of the soldier whose back I was on in the picture. I met him in Japan, in Sapporo, when I went in 1995. A year later the soldier died. The people who brought me to Japan brought the soldier to Sapporo. He didn't speak English but had a translator. The only reason the soldier was alive was because before the battle of Attu, he was captured in China[10] and became a POW. He was a POW until the war ended.

The picture shows me as a kid, and the soldier has me on his back. We weren't close friends. The picture came out in Japan somehow and stories were created about the photo. I didn't know the picture was even taken until Sam came to Atka. They knew it was me because I was the only kid that age on Attu. Somehow they knew my name. When I was in Japan, every morning I would see my picture on TV and in the newspaper, so I went down to the front desk at the hotel, and they cut out the article for me. I really wanted to know what it said.

---

9   Masami Sugiyama invited Nick to Japan, personally funded the trip, and arranged the meeting between Nick and the former soldier, Mr. Kanami.

10   According to Masami Sugiyama, Mr. Kanami was captured in Siberia.

REFLECTIONS ON LIFE IN ATKA

In Attu and Atka, the temperature never goes below zero, but the wind chill does go below zero here in the Aleutian Islands. They both have deep-water harbors. The Atka harbor doesn't ever freeze. Ever since I can remember, the waterline has been creeping up. The temperature gets warmer every year. There are only four trees on all of Atka Island. They were planted after the war.

In Atka, our houses never had insulation. They were just made out of wood and all open underneath, not a single piece of insulation in the house. During the winter, it got cold inside, but my family and I were used to it. Sometimes in the morning when I got up, if there was water in a cup, it would be frozen. We would have to get up early in the morning to light the wood stove. The wood stove did not take long to heat the house. We never had a refrigerator or freezer, so during the winter, after we would go hunting, the food would last longer than in the summer. In the summer, we would have to eat it up right away or throw it away before it spoiled. Aleuts do not waste anything. We use everything that we hunt. For example, during the summer, we would use fish traps in the creek and after we get all the fish we want, we would let the rest go so they can spawn. February and March used to be a tough time for us Aleuts since we did not have a freezer to put away food, only salted salmon and dried and smoked fish.

Atka has two active volcanoes on the north end. One is called Korovin, and the other one is Atka volcano. In Atka there are lots of harbors, creeks, and lakes. At every creek, there used to be a mud house where the fish came up. People were scattered all around Atka and Amlia. On Amlia there used to be a village at the first harbor, right across the pass. I know this because I was trapping there one time and from up above, I saw two or three big mud houses that used to be there, plus around it there were little ones. There must have been quite a few people that lived there. Way before the war, people buried their dead in the caves. There are two caves in Atka that have skulls in them, and some by the camp where there are buried people.

I do not know when the people moved their village, but they used to have a village on Korovin side that is now called Old Harbor. There never was a Russian settlement on Atka. In the 1880 census, the village was called Nazan. The population was 236. Atka had its own post office in 1938, and in 1957 had the post office in the store.

I lived about six years in Attu and a little over three years in Japan, and the rest of my life in Atka. I do not want to disappoint anybody by saying something about the Aleutians that I don't know too much about. I have not been all over Atka. I have discovered most of it but not all. I am sure people have lived here on Atka before the Russians did. What I do not like is that we Alaskans owned and lived on this land and Russia came around and sold it to the United States, and now we have to buy it back from the United States. The US Fish and Wildlife Service owns Atka except for the private lands.

Growing Up and Going to School

In Attu there were no children my age. Most of the kids were older. So when the war started, I used to walk between the Japanese military men, and they treated me nice. On the way back from Japan, I did the same thing with the United States soldiers. When I got to Atka I found some kids my age, so we played together; we walked around together and did everything together.

When I was a kid, on my birthdays I never had a cake or presents. The only thing I remember on my birthdays was that I went to Russian Orthodox church on December 19th every year. The only other thing I remember on my birthday is that I felt good; I don't know why. I never had a cake till I got about thirty-five years old. That's when my wife, Vasha, started making me homemade cake.

While in Attu and Japan, I never went to school. All I knew was the Aleut language, and a little Japanese. When I got to Atka I started school. I was ten years old and was in kindergarten. I was uneducated and I did not know the alphabet or numbers. I did not mind it much but when I started, I did not like to color. Later, I started coloring better. Soon I started reading, but the pronunciation was hard for me. For example, when "island" came up I would say "is-land" instead of the proper way, and all the other kids started laughing. The teacher told them to stop since they did the same thing with other words. I felt better after that.

When I was a kid going to school, one of the teachers took us out to the first creek on the right side of the village and had us dig right above the creek. We dug and found some spears and a few other items, but I do not know what happened to them and cannot recall the teacher's name. If you don't see a person or do things that you used to do, you forget. I used to be able to speak, sing, and count in Japanese but can't anymore since I don't use it often.

I don't have a high school degree. When I turned eighteen, the school didn't want me anymore. I tried to go back three times but they kicked me out because of my age. On the third time, they got my mom and the chief of the village, and told them that I should not go back to school anymore, so I did not. I taught myself after that. I read everything I could. I mostly learned from the elders. Some of the elders never went to school, and I felt they were the smartest. Their education was learning from life.

Some of the seniors still write in Aleut, but most kids today do not speak our language anymore. They have to be taught in school. I teach Aleut in school to the kids. Attu and Atka have different dialects. They have the same words but slightly different meaning.

Left Behind by the Military

When the military left Atka, they left a lot of rifle and machine gun ammunition, but we could not see them because they were halfway buried or inside bunkers. When some kids and I found them, we would play with them. We used to take the tip off the shell and pour the powder into a beer can and light it and watch it fly around. The military left a whole bunch of dynamite caps that we used to play with, using a twelve-volt battery to make them pop. Some of them make a small pop, and it takes a while before they kick off. The first time I picked up one after it did not pop, it popped suddenly, and I got part of it in my leg and ear.

In Attu, the Japanese also left ammo, especially in caves, and there were a lot of caves on Attu. Later in the years, I went back to Attu to work for a salvage company from Tacoma. We salvaged lots of military stuff that they left behind from Adak, Kiska, and Attu. When I was in Attu salvaging military stuff, I did not go to the village side because I was working long hours and did not have time. I used to work from morning until evening. I did not even go to where we used to have summer camp, but I could see it from the road.

After we got back from the war, here in Atka the only transportation was by military plane or military barge that brought supplies. The only way to fly out of Atka was to fly to Adak. Later on, Reeve started flying in, but the military airport that was made out of metal matting rotted away, and sand started piling on the airport. Reeve quit flying here. Since then, the only transportation we had was a military tug from Adak that brought mail once a month.

On May 31, 2004, Memorial Day, I was watching the news and they were talking about veterans. I was wondering if I'm a veteran or not because I was shot at when I was six years old, even though I never joined the military. I had to register for the draft, but there was no post office in Atka that time to register with. I did not know how to register, so I did not. After I got married, they just put a post office in the village, and I registered. They asked why I did not register when I was eighteen and I told them why. They gave me some kind of card. The reason I gave for not registering is that I was a prisoner of war for more than three years.

Working Life

Before and after the war, we used to saw and chop wood all the time. I used to do that almost every day, and it was hard work, but it kept me healthy. Right now I am still working. After the war, I started working in the Pribilofs. I must have worked at least thirteen summers there. That is where I learned my trade as a plumber, electrician, and carpenter helper, and later, on my own, I learned mechanical work. Right now, I am working at the school as school maintenance. I am doing all right now. I have done all kinds of work. I never found anything that I could not do. I used to apply for any jobs that I could find to make some money for a living.

When I got old enough to work, I got my first job in the Pribilofs, St. Paul Island, working on fur seals. I was fifteen in 1950 when I started working in St. Paul. I didn't take my birth certificate to Japan, and I didn't have it. They made me apply for a Social Security card when I worked on St. Paul. It took a month to get one, even though all the paperwork was done in St. Paul. I worked for the sealing operation in the summer for thirteen to fifteen years. I worked for the government and was paid $1.25 per hour. I did different jobs while working there. A lot of times, my job was blubbering seals—taking the blubber off the skins. The meat was either ground or cooked into fertilizer. They fed it to mink in mink farms.

I got a better job working for the Tacoma Salvage Company. I cleaned debris left from World War II on Adak, Attu, and Amchitka. Other workers cleaned in Shemya. I cleaned copper, iron, lead, batteries, and drones. They salvaged whatever they could. I learned how to operate a Cat. A metal barge took everything that was salvaged to Seattle or Tacoma. On Adak, some Japanese ships took car engines.

After that, I took any job I could find. I used to work as a carpenter and I fished. Sometimes we got hired from outside, so I went out and worked on fish processors, and then fished in Kodiak, and now I am fishing halibut here in Atka. This is how I ended up with a twenty-two-foot aluminum boat and eighteen-foot aluminum boat and still have them.

I fished in Kodiak twenty-five to twenty-six years ago. I only fished in the summer, for pink, red, and silver salmon. I crewed on boats that were captained by people from Atka, who ran the boats for Seattle companies. The captains knew me from Atka. I got paid a crew share—the pay depended on how many pounds of fish we caught. There was a two- or three-man crew, mostly three, including the captain and two deckhands. The fishing boat was thirty-two feet. I was in charge of the power skiff. Using the skiff, I would create a 200–250 yard circle with the net. We used to fish all around Kodiak. The company had tenders to take the fish from the boats to the cannery. Port Williams was the base for the boats in the winter.

I worked on a crab processor. I don't think crab was a traditional Aleut food. When I was young I never saw a crab because they lived in too deep water. Now crabs come into shallower waters. One time I caught crab by accident on a halibut hook when the crab grabbed the bait and wouldn't let go.

Right now, I have been working for the school district and the airport. I have a little contract with the airport to remove snow on the airstrip, and I work as a janitor and do maintenance at the school for twenty-one years now. I am still working but not making too much money, just enough to live comfortably.

When I was growing up, I was poor and hungry. After the war, when I got here, I had no socks, no heavy jacket, no boots; I could not afford it. My shoes had holes in them, but even then I still packed wood in the snow with my feet freezing. But right now, I feel that I have too much. I have a freezer, I'm working; the only reason that I have money is that I want to retire and pay for bills, like credit card bills. In addition, I need to pay for my phone bill, light bill, and monthly payment on my house.

Earlier in life, I had a couple of friends with the Democratic and Republican parties, and they both say that the Republicans help the rich and the Democrats help the poor. I don't know if that is true or not, but when President Bush cut taxes I thought I was going to get some tax cut, but since I don't make much money I didn't get much of a tax break. This is why I believe there is some truth to that saying.

Hunting, Fishing, and Wildlife

Out here in the Aleutians, everything is expensive. Almost everything is tripled in price from Anchorage or Seattle. Therefore, we had to survive like the old-timers. They know how to survive. When we were young, a friend and I were in a creek trying to catch some silver salmon. One of the silvers went under the bank. We had a hook on a stick trying to hook them out, and we never made it. An elder came around and asked us if there was fish under the bank and we said, "Yes, but we can't catch it." He went and put his hook upwards. We had our hook downwards, and that is why we could not catch any.

The tide here in the Aleutians doesn't go low as the tide in the mainland. I used to fish in Kodiak, and I know the tide there goes sometimes twelve feet lower than normal, and here in Atka it goes six or seven feet only. In Kodiak sometimes you see a boat on top of the rock about twelve feet up in the air, and when we go under the bridge people up there looked down at us and smile.

Anyway, I'm a good shot for hunting seals and ducks and sea lions, things like that. I got good because we did not have enough ammo. The older people used to give me one or two shells and told me to get something to eat, and I couldn't afford to miss, so I really got to be a good shot.

You cannot go out anytime you want on a skiff because of the weather. The weather out here in the Aleutians is nasty. It is usually very windy, sometimes foggy and wet. The winters do not get freezing cold, but the summers do not get very hot, either. Even in bad weather, people like to hunt. I enjoy hunting whenever I can. I do not do much hunting anymore because my aiming eye is not good anymore and I cannot see that well.

I want to say something about wildlife. They say that wildlife is disappearing. When I used to fish for halibut, I saw dead birds floating around, and these birds are from out in the ocean. They are not land birds, or at least not birds from Atka anyway. I think the reason that these birds were dying is from oil. People do not respect wildlife as much as they did in the past. I see people throw trash in the ocean. People should worry about what the future will lead to if this keeps happening. Wildlife get beached up here on the island and end up dying—whales, sea lions, birds, and sea otters. There is a lot of fishing here in Atka like king crab, black cod, grey cod, king salmon, pink salmon, halibut, and many more. Sometimes during the summer, the halibut are so close to the beach you can catch them. Almost year-round there, fishermen stop by from other parts of Alaska while fishing.

I know a few people that are afraid of killer whales. Killer whales do not bother anybody. Sometimes they would follow you around and get close to your boat, but they do not do anything. One time an old-timer said that when he had a seal on top of his kayak, the killer whale would take it but would not bother him.

One time I was on an island near Atka where seagulls nest. After the eggs hatched, I saw some eagles killing small seagulls, and I figured there would be lot of small ones left, but there were only a few. I never get tired of watching wildlife. When I go out, I see eagles, crows, seagulls, ptarmigans, horned puffins, fish, etc. When I was a kid I raised an eaglet, but I couldn't keep it as a pet because it was too mean. There are some birds in Atka that we have never seen before. When I was a kid there used to be a few birds, but now there are a whole lot around.

For the past five years now, the reindeer, during the winter, would come down the hills to the village. The reindeer would stay around the village for almost the whole winter because there is more food around near the village than there is in the hills. I was told that six or twelve reindeer were put on Atka before the war. Now there are thousands. During the war the reindeer population grew, and now there are maybe about two or three thousand reindeer here on the island of Atka.

One thing about Atka is that Atka has all kinds of decorated, different colored rocks. In certain areas there are different kinds of rocks. Atka is beautiful when you're up in the hills. I used to walk eight, ten, twelve hours a day hunting for reindeer before the ATV four-wheelers came around. The reindeer were introduced before the war, and now there are thousands of them. It is beautiful up there in the hills during the winter or summer, especially during the summer when it is all green. There are hills, lots of lakes, valleys, creeks, and rivers. Mostly there are big hills, and when you walk, you practically—you have to climb up them. Looking for reindeer, I would go up on the highest hills and look around. When I spotted them, I would walk toward them, and when they were too far, I used to herd them closer to the village when I was alone. When you're by yourself, animals are not scared of you, even sea lions, ducks, and seals. When you are alone in the boat, they come close to you, but when there are two of you, they don't do that. I do not understand that. When there are two of you, the reindeer get kind of spooky, but when you're alone, it's easier to herd them. When they are so far from the village, they do not want to be herded anymore and try to go back. I used to shoot one there, pack it, and drag it home.

There is a lot of driftwood around the island. After the war, the driftwood has been used for firewood. I use cottonwood driftwood to smoke fish. The village areas have been picked clean. I have found unopened beer cans, flares, sometimes you find packaged food. I used to find a lot of Japanese [glass] balls after World War II, washed up on the shore.

Atka Is Far Away from Anywhere Else

The state of Alaska built an airport in Atka twenty-two years ago. PenAir has a mail contract with the state to fly mail to Atka three times a week from Dutch Harbor. The plane can also carry seven to nine people, or cargo. The plane used to take seafood out, but now it's too expensive. Now we have Coastal Transportation, a boat that comes three times a summer to pick up halibut and black cod. It leaves with two hundred thousand pounds of frozen fish.

I still live here in Atka. I never owned a house. I still don't own one but I'm buying one from Aleutian Housing Authority right now and hope to own it in a few years. You are supposed to live in the house for twenty-five years to own it. It was a prebuilt house. They brought the two halves in and put them together in Atka.

Not many people live here. I estimate around a hundred people live in Atka year-round. More come in the summer so they can fish. In Atka we live with the wildlife. The reindeer come down to the village. Sea lions go by here. People in Atka still eat seal and sea lions. We have halibut and codfish come close to shore. Before sea otters came around, we used to have crab on the beaches. In summertime, all the creeks around the island are full of salmon, and we do not get any tourists out here. It is hard to get out here when the weather is bad. The only transportation out here is by PenAir, from Dutch Harbor to Atka. The plane is supposed to arrive to Atka twice a week, but sometimes we do not get any planes for two weeks, or more, because of the weather.

After the war when we got to Atka, I used to watch people build skiffs, and then I built me one. After my first year in St. Paul, I had a little bit of money and all that I needed to buy was a hammer and a handsaw. The rest of the stuff came from the old military buildings, like nails, paint, and plywood. I had to buy some cork and cotton. I built me a fourteen-foot boat. I had to buy oars since I did not have a motor. Once that was built, I started going out on my own. The first time I went out in my boat, I hand-lined for halibut, and that time there were many halibut around.

In my time, I sank with my skiff three times. It was always near shore and always due to rough seas. The first time, it was nice out, and I had a skiff full of driftwood for my stove. I tried to fit into a northwest wind blowing about forty, and a couple of waves just sank me. My motor quit since it was underwater, so I had to paddle back to a calmer place, and pulled my boat, and walked home in a wet snow that night and got home about three in the morning. The second time, a friend and I were out halibut fishing, hand-lining, and the wind started blowing southeast about forty, and on the way back we sank again. When we sank, everything we had, even the halibut, was floating in the water, so we headed for the beach, but just before we got to the beach the motor quit, so we jumped in the water and pulled our boat in and saved what we could save, and we walked home. The third time, I was out getting driftwood for my stove, and it was blowing northwest about thirty to forty. We were just outside the village. I had too much wood in my boat, so I started sinking and headed toward the beach, but this time the motor didn't quit. Nowadays I use GPS in my boat for fishing.

Atka is a beautiful place to live, but it is very expensive. I pay over six hundred dollars a month for fuel, three hundred a month for electricity, and pay for rent on our home every month, phone bills, grocery, oil, etc. If we did not live off the land, I do not think we could have been able to make it. The reason why it is so expensive here is that we live so far west of the mainland. It costs a lot to have everything either flown in or brought in by boat.

There are not many jobs on Atka. There is fishing during the summer. The school district, the store, and the post office all hire some people. There is a health aide at the clinic. Some people have jobs working for Aleutian Housing or the telephone company. The guy who works as the diesel operator doesn't make any money. The city of Atka owns and operates the gas storage tanks. In 2007, a gallon of gas was over five dollars.

The Atka airport has three thousand feet of paved runway and is a hundred feet wide. The city wants a longer runway, but it's too expensive to lengthen it. PenAir comes in with a twin-engine prop on a regular flight from Dutch Harbor. There are charters to Atka. One time a Northern Air Cargo DC6 landed, a four-engine cargo plane. It was flying in bait for the processors. It was completely empty when it left.

Our small dock for cargo, a newly built road from the village to the dock, and the main dock are all on the other side of the bay. When I wrote this on June 14, 2004, we were finally starting to see king salmon in Atka. Some people from the village were commercially fishing halibut right then.

When you decide to come to Atka, make sure you schedule longer than you expect because of the weather. What I am trying to say is that when people come to Atka, and they are ready to head back out, the plane is often delayed and does not arrive until a day or two later.

Learning from the Elders

I learned many things from the old-timers. They taught me how to survive and taught me how to be good, told me what is good and bad. Nowadays, the younger kids do not seem like they're interested in that stuff anymore. Since they have everything, they think it is going to be like that all the time, so they don't care. Later on, when they get older and their parents cannot support them anymore, they are going to have a hard time. I hope they read my book and learn from it.

Old-timers used to tell me that "what you do on your birthday, you get good at," and I never believed it until now. If you work or do something on your birthday, you do get real good at it. It happened to me. Most things that old-timers told me I did not believe, but most of them came true. When I was young, I used to camp and trap with old-timers during the summer and winter, and they used to tell me stories. I do not know how to say this, but the elders predicted the future, and there are many things that I was told were going to happen or happened already. Few of those old-timers knew how to read or write, but they knew what was going on and knew what they were talking about.

The old-timers used to tell me that the Russians were tough, mean, and killed a lot of people. The old-timers that told me many stories are all gone. I have learned a lot from them. The reason why I was with the old-timers all the time is because I was kicked out of school when I was eighteen, so I spent my time with them since there was nothing much to do. The old-timers did not talk much about how they got here. I am thinking maybe they did not know or that they were here from the beginning. One other thing that an old-timer told me is that if you live in a warm, sunny, calm environment, that you will pay for it later. What I mean by this is it will get rough like hurricanes, floods, etc. If you have too perfect of a place to live, too disastrous of a thing will happen. If you live in a place like the Aleutians, the weather is usually bad and stays the same but there are times when it is very nice. Like I said, the summers here are not too hot, and the winters are not too cold. Usually it is just windy, foggy, and damp.

When I was young, I hardly ever wanted to be inside. I am usually always outside. Whenever the elders went camping or went out in a boat, I used to volunteer to go with them to help them out. They told many stories about the past, and sometimes they told a story about what would happen. Some stories that they told were that the world was going to change. I do not know how they would know about that. They said that the ocean is going to come up every year, and now I see it happening. In addition, they said there would be more wind and not as many earthquakes, and now that I am older, it is happening. They used to tell me when it was nice all the time and no wind, there are a lot of little earthquakes. One time I was walking and I did not feel the earthquake, but I saw the land wavy-like. Later on, when I reached the village, the elders told me there was an earthquake. They told me that the world would end sometime and not too far away.

They also mentioned that the children would start going against their parents. The kids would not listen, and now I am seeing it happening. The parents cannot control their children because the government made a law saying we cannot spank our children, and if we did, we would either end up in jail or be separated from our families. A long time ago, if one kid did something wrong, everybody was spanked. That is how we controlled our kids. For hunting and fishing, the elders told me not to kill or take anything that I do not need. They asked me to control the wildlife. They never wasted anything that is edible. For example, when they would shoot the geese, they would pluck the whole head and eat it, but I never tried it because there was no meat on the head.

What I was told when I was younger was that if you have an easy life, you pay for it later. They told me to be satisfied for what I have and what I get and not complain. If you ask for things you do not need or take more than you need and complain, you will be sorry later. I learned that when you fix something in a hurry, you end up doing it again, but if you take your time, you're finished on that first try.

When I was young, I was told to respect elders, teachers, doctors, and priests. We had a chief in the village, and when the chief said anything, the vice chief went around the houses and told the people what was going to happen or what we needed to do. For example, if we needed to clean the village, everyone helped, and if the kids did anything wrong we were spanked, even if we did not do anything. Even after the war, I was told to help others and not ask for help, so I used to help others, even when I was a kid, and even when I did not have food or anything. The elders did not have much to give me in return, so they said that I will do better later in life, and that I am right now. Another thing old-timers told me was that when you walk, don't drink water, and that's how I used to be. I used to walk all day, sometimes eight to twelve hours without water, and never get tired. Once I got home, I would drink water and get tired out, so I believe what they told me.

Everybody in Attu and Atka goes to church, or used to. I hardly go to church anymore because an elder told me, "If you go to church just to think or just for amusement, you might as well not go at all and just stay home and pray, where there are no distractions." This is why I don't bother. I also believe God is everywhere, and he can hear you pray no matter where you are.

When I said I saw Jesus just before the morning the Japanese landed, an old-timer told me that kids see what adults can't see. I believed him because I saw Jesus come down. He did not touch the ground, but He blessed me and then when I turned around to see if anyone was watching, Jesus was gone. I also said I saw a ghost one evening. It was the shape of a person and I could see right through it. That next morning someone died.

Relatives from Attu

I came back from Japan with my two uncles, Innokenty Golodoff and Willy Golodoff. My uncles told me some stories about Attu afterward. When I was growing up, I used to ask my mom about Japan but she never wanted to talk about it. I think my brother wants to forget about Japan also. I was always interested about what happened throughout my childhood, but no one really wanted to talk about it. I am always interested. I think Japan was a nice place to live when I was staying there.

I had cousins, uncles, and aunts on Attu, but I don't know a lot about them. My mother died from diabetes at Alaska Native Medical Center in Anchorage while I was thirty or forty and living in Atka, and her body was sent back to Atka. The only Attuans left are my younger brother, Greg; my younger sister, Elizabeth; and me. My older brother John died last year. Greg Golodoff lives in Atka, and Elizabeth Kudrin lives in Anchorage. My brother and sister don't like to talk about Japan.

That is all I know from Attu. Children of Attu people are still around, but most of them are not living in Atka. I do not even know how many there are. I know one living here in Atka is about all.

I don't know if my older brother and sister were in school when we were taken to Japan, but I think they must have been. My older brother lived in Atka. He died in August 2009. John didn't like to talk about what happened because he didn't keep track of what was going on. He was six to eight years older than me. I didn't know him very well, and after the war he didn't come back to Atka with us. John went to school at Mt. Edgecombe. He came back to the Aleutians and started to work on the *North Star*. One day, the *North Star* came to Atka, and John got off and stayed for a while. He left to go find a job on a fishing boat. He came back to live on Atka six years ago.

My brother Greg joined the Army. Then he lived in Anchorage and worked there. I took Greg to work on a processor. After that, Greg moved to Atka, where he still lives.

I was married to my wife for over fifty years, and I have eight kids with her, four boys and four girls. One of the girls passed away not too long ago, but she left a beautiful little granddaughter, Niki. All my kids are grown up and do not live with us anymore. My son Raymond lives in Anchorage and is a school bus driver. He moved to Anchorage three years ago to find work.

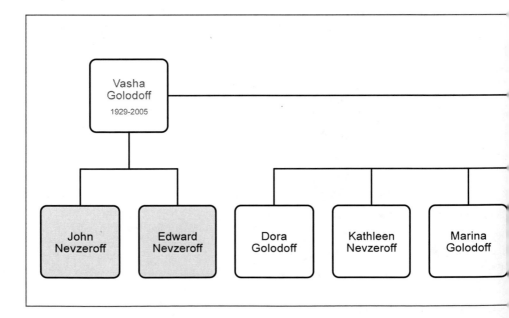

FIG. 5. Nick's children. *Adapted from Family Echo www.familyecho.com*

Elizabeth and Gregory Golodoff in Atka in 1946-1947. *University of Washington Press, Ethel Ross Oliver*

The reason I'm writing this book is to tell you about how Aleuts were back then, how my life back then got me to where I am now, how I learned, and what happened during the war. There is little info about Attu and Atka out there. Hardly anyone knows about the islands or Aleuts. The Aleuts today all turned modern.

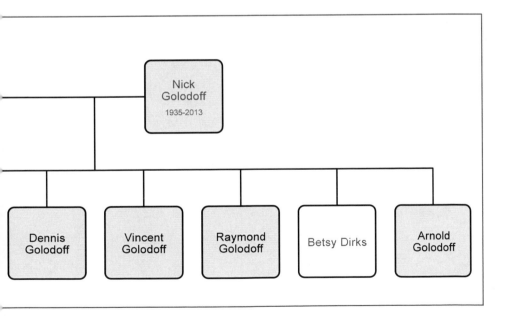

COMMENTARY AND
FIRST-PERSON ACCOUNTS

Attu before the War

In 1942, before the war began, Attu was a nice, quiet place with a population of about thirty-four people. We had nothing, no insulation in the houses, and no inside plumbing. There was a woodstove to heat the house. Attu was plain and quiet all the time.

—Nick Golodoff

Nick's memories of Attu as a quiet and pleasant place to live are reaffirmed by numerous other sources, such as officers on coast guard vessels, teachers hired by the Bureau of Indian Affairs, and visitors such as a Scottish botanist and a stray American archaeologist. The village was praised for its harmony and industry. Some of the outsiders theorized that because of its isolation, Attu had escaped many unsavory worldly influences.

Before World War II, there was little exchange of cash on Attu. The villagers obtained most of their food from hunting, fishing, and gathering. Sea lions, seals, and salmon were the main staples of the diet (BIA 1988:27, 65). Salmon was plentiful. The main summer fish camp was several miles from the winter village, at Sarana Bay, near the river mouth. People used driftwood for firewood, and sometimes they had to travel long distances to find it. Occasionally walrus showed up, and the men sold the ivory (Wright 1988).

In winter, the Attuans trapped fox on nearby Agattu Island. Teacher Etta Jones wrote to her family in 1941 that the Attuans' main source of income was from trapping blue fox. She reported that the trappers pooled their furs and divided

Two aerial views of Chichagof Harbor and Attu Village taken at the beginning of the Battle of Attu. Both are dated May 14, 1943, about eight months after the Attuans had been taken to Japan in September 1942. *US Air Force [top], US Navy, courtesy Dirk Spennemann [bottom]*

the cash received among all residents, including widows, orphans, and others who were unable to trap for themselves (Breu 2009:151). The women wove baskets for sale to outsiders. At the village store, the Attuans traded furs and baskets for goods such as flour, tea, coal, and kerosene.

Beginning in the early 1920s, Fred Schroeder, a non-Native trader working for the Alaska Commercial Company, spent part of each year on Attu Island (Jones 1946:39). The commanding officer of the Coast Guard cutter *Tallapoosa* noted that, with the exception of a few old women who stayed in the village to take care of the houses, almost all the other residents of Attu left in August to trap blue fox on other islands, particularly Agattu, during the winter. The date of the villagers' departure depended on the arrival of the Alaska Commercial Company schooner *Eunice* in mid-August (US Coast Guard 1931).

Attu did not get very many visitors, but the village made a big impression on those who did manage to stop there. In the summer of 1936, Alan G. May, an amateur archaeologist who had been part of famed anthropologist Aleš Hrdlička's expedition that year, spent a month in the village. May was put up in the large, modern schoolhouse, which was not being used (Stein n.d.:3). He wrote that the settlement's structures included a church, a schoolhouse, about a dozen wood-frame houses, and the same number of barabaras still in use. He had been told that as late as 1928, everyone in the village lived in barabaras (May 1936:96).

Naturalist Isobel Hutchinson visited Attu the same year as Alan May, after

"Maggie's barabara." *Alan G. May papers, Archives and Special Collections, Consortium Library, University of Alaska Anchorage*

several weeks of botanical collection in the Aleutians. She said that on Attu, "Back of the beach were a few old barabaras covered with flowers and turf, but the islanders now occupy comfortable little wooden houses such as might be seen in any other part of Alaska" (Hutchinson 1937:170). Hutchinson had already heard good things about the village from the officers of the coast guard cutter who took her to the island. She wrote that coast guard officers had told her:

> The natives of Attu . . . are by far the happiest and best of all the natives, because they live in such a remote situation and bad influences don't so easily come their way. They know this themselves and don't want to be brought into closer touch with the world. They are always the most friendly and helpful too, coming down to meet us and lending a hand if required. (Hutchinson 1937:168)

One of the main sources of information about life in Attu in the 1930s comes from the records of the coast guard cutters that stopped at the island to bring mail and supplies and provide medical and dental services. For example, the *Haida* and the *Chelan* both visited Attu in September 1930. The *Haida* treated people with conjunctivitis, bronchitis, myalgia, tuberculosis, and pleurisy. The commanding officer of the *Chelan* wrote, "The medical officer of the *Chelan* was sent ashore to the village and gave medical aid to seventeen natives and left a supply of medicines for their use during the coming winter season" (US Coast Guard 1930:2).

In 1939, while he was ashore, the commanding officer of the *Itasca* married two couples (Willie and Julia Golodoff and Alex and Elizabeth Prossoff), performed other judicial acts, and recorded the six deaths that had occurred in the village since the coast guard's last visit. The ship found nine people on Attu in need of medical assistance and five in need of dental work. The dental report for the trip told of pulling teeth from two people; others were lucky enough to receive only an examination. The medical party's census counted twenty-one Native males, fourteen Native females, eight children, two white males, and one white female in the village population (US Coast Guard 1939).[11]

The coast guard officers got to know Vassa "Maggie" Prokopeuff, a basket maker, whom they called "The Rock of Ages." She is mentioned frequently in the records of visitors to Attu who bought baskets from her and commissioned her to weave special ones.

The most well known Attu resident of the twentieth century, however, was Mike Hodikoff, chief of the village when it was occupied by the Japanese in 1942.

---

[11] One of the white males was probably the trader, Fred Schroeder. The other white man and woman may have been teachers who stayed for a few weeks at Attu one summer.

Hodikoff was born on Attu in 1893 and brought to Unalaska as an orphan in 1910, staying first at the Methodist orphanage, the Jesse Lee Home, and later with relatives. He returned to Attu and married Anesia (sometimes called Anastasia) Prokopeuff in 1920. Educated in Unalaska, he spoke better English than other Attu residents. English was still rarely spoken in Attu, but Hodikoff spoke it well and very rapidly (May 1936:101). In addition to being chief, Hodikoff was also a lay reader in church (where he also spoke rapidly) and had the job of sending in weather reports.

Hodikoff was already a village leader in the early 1930s, when references to him appear in coast guard reports. The US Coast Guard was devoting special attention to Attu because Japanese fishing vessels were suspected in the area. Vicious storms at Attu in 1931 wrecked the coast guard station there and three barabaras, including one belonging to Hodikoff, whose six-year-old son was killed in the storm. Hodikoff lost another child when his young daughter Mary Hodikoff (also age six) was taken to Unalaska for medical treatment and died during an operation to remove her tonsils (US Coast Guard 1931:3–6). His wife died before World War II, leaving him with three children: Angelina, Stephen, and George.

In 1936, Mike Hodikoff communicated with the outside world using Attu's wireless radio station. In the summer of 1934, a fleet of navy ships was sent to

Basket weaver on Attu. Maggie Prokopeuff. *UAF, Murie Family Papers*

TOP: The 'Rock of Ages,' center, and two other Natives. CENTER: Agefangel on left, Mike and Anastasia [Anesia] with a group from the village out collecting roots. BOTTOM: Chief Mike Hodikoff and his son Gorga eating lunch when out searching for drift wood at Holtz Bay.

All images this page from the Alan G. May papers, Archives and Special Collections, Consortium Library, University of Alaska Anchorage survey the Aleutian Islands. During that time, the navy erected a temporary radio station in the school building at Attu, and the radio men may have taught the chief to transmit messages. Alan May observed that when the coast guard came to town, all the villagers came aboard the ship to watch movies (May 1942:135).

May wrote that Schroeder, the trader at Attu, supported the village inhabitants in several ways. He paid Mike Hodikoff sixty cents an hour to work for him and left him in charge of the store when Schroeder was out of town. Schroeder's wife, too, contributed to the welfare of the people there. May wrote,

> Mrs. Schroeder sent a dress as a gift to each woman on the island,
> which seems very nice of her, and she also sent toys for the kiddies.
> Mrs. Schroeder has never visited the island, but she does this once
> a year. (May 1936:122)

Furthermore, Schroeder helped the Attuans pay for construction of the new church by advancing them money for lumber against their season's fox trapping. The old church had been a grass-roofed barabara (May 1936:118). The women of Attu also raised money for the new church by selling baskets in Unalaska

"Anastasia [Anesia], the chief's wife." *Alan G. May papers, Archives and Special Collections, Consortium Library, University of Alaska Anchorage*

"Baskets and Weavers, Attu, Alaska." The girl on the right is Anesia Prokopeuff, who became Chief Mike Hodikoff's wife. *UAF, Murie family photos*

(Shapsnikoff and Hudson 1974:41). May noted that when Schroeder arrived in late July 1936, all the residents were pleased to see him, and he seemed like a nice man (May 1936:129).

The school was built in 1932, but it would be almost a decade before any teachers were persuaded to come to Attu for longer than brief summertime visits (Kohlhoff 1995:6). Etta Jones arrived in 1941 to serve as a permanent teacher. Her husband, Foster Jones, assumed the duty of radio operator for the village. Both were sixty-two years old and had worked in other schools in Alaska (Breu 2009:149).

Prewar Fears and Clues about Japanese Invasion

Japanese presence was observed or suspected in Attu and other Near Islands since the first decades of the twentieth century. Mike Hodikoff recalled that sometime around 1910, Japanese marauders had stolen fox skins from the Attuans and that they killed his father in the struggle that followed (Jones 1946:40). This may have been one of the incidents Nick Golodoff refers to when he mentions the trappers who didn't return.

Beginning in the early 1930s, the US military was watchful in the Aleutian Islands. The navy sent a fleet of ships with amphibious aircraft to survey the Aleutians in the summer of 1934. As early as 1937, the coast guard officer on the *Haida* reported that on the way back from Attu the boat hands were "constantly checking for 'Jap ships' in fishing grounds." In August of 1938, when the *Cyane*

The old church. "Greek church on Attu Island, the furtherest [sic] point west."
UAF, Wickersham State Historic Site

The new church, built in 1932. "From the church looking down the main street. View of a wooden plank pathway to the church, with orthodox crosses marking graves on the right."
Alan G. May papers, Archives and Special Collections, Consortium Library, University of Alaska Anchorage

Attu Natives, M.G.7/41. LEFT: This is likely Annie Borenin, who became Mike Hodikoff's second wife, with her son Victor. She was also Nick Golodoff's father's sister. *Alaska State Library, Evelyn Butler and George Dale*

visited Attu, it also scouted along Holtz Bay, looking for evidence of Japanese occupancy (US Coast Guard 1939).

When Etta Jones was assigned to teach in Attu, she and her husband, Foster Jones, knew there was danger of an attack from the Japanese. When boat operators Don and Ginger Pickard visited Attu in April 1942, Foster Jones told them that if the Japanese came, he would destroy his radio and the island's supplies of gasoline and oil. He was also training ("drilling") the Attu men to protect their home (Stein n.d.:4-6). Etta Jones wrote in a letter that the American flag flew proudly above the village and that the Attuans disliked and distrusted the Japanese (Kohlhoff 1995:40).

Nick Golodoff recalls that when he was a little boy, people talked about hearing mysterious footsteps and finding other traces of prewar visitors to Attu. Some people thought they were boogiemen, but later there was speculation that they were Japanese. The Attuans knew of the Japanese interest in the Aleutians, and they had already had encounters with Japanese fishing vessels and fur poachers. Alan May wrote in his journal that a captain of the coast guard had told him that "Attu has been completely surveyed by the Japs under the pretext of collecting flowers and butterflies (without permission) and the natives cowed into not speaking about it" (May 1936:90). The chief of the village, Mike Hodikoff, told a visitor to Attu that personnel from the Japanese navy had already been in the area to take measurements and soundings in the harbors (Stein n.d.:5). On land, he said, they had left behind stakes with Japanese characters (Nutchuk [Simeon Oliver] 1946:148). In May 1942, the US Navy took Chief Hodikoff and Alfred Prokopeuff, the second chief, on board the seaplane tender USS *Casco* so the local men could show them likely shore landing spots.

Mike Hodikoff on board the *Casco*. *Aleutian-Pribilof Island Association*

The Japanese Invasion, June 7, 1942

The Japanese bombed Dutch Harbor on June 3 and 4, 1942. On Attu, in the early morning of June 7, Foster Jones sent his usual weather report by radio. Charles Magee, teacher and radio operator on Atka, heard Jones say he had a hunch the Japanese were going to attack Attu. The radio went dead after that (Stein n.d.:8).

As the Japanese forces approached Attu, they split up, and the larger force got lost. On the night of June 7, 1942, the Attu residents heard the Japanese boats coming into Holtz Bay, on the west side of the island. A contingent of soldiers came into the village on foot the next morning. It was Sunday morning and the attack surprised the Attuans as they left church (Carter 1994:35).

> The Japanese poured out of the hills west of the village, yelling and shooting. The frightened Aleuts ran to their homes. Rifle fire randomly struck the houses. At least two Aleuts were slightly wounded, one of them, Annie Hodikoff, the chief's wife,[12] shot in

---

[12]   Actually, it was chief Mike Hodikoff's brother Fred Hodikoff's wife, Annie, who was shot in the leg. Annie Hodikoff was twenty-three, about the same age as Annie Borenin, who became Mike Hodikoff's common-law second wife.

the leg. Some of the younger Aleuts wanted to get their rifles and
defend their homes and families. (Stein n.d.:8)

An older man counseled the young men that they were outnumbered and would
never prevail. Six men, including Innokenty Golodoff, ran away to the hills and
stayed there all day (Golodoff 1966). Later the Japanese sent other Unangan residents to bring them back.

The Unangan residents were gathered in the schoolhouse, and Foster and Etta
Jones were questioned separately. The Japanese distributed mimeographed papers
and announced to the Native population of the village that they were liberated
from the American oppressors. After the soldiers searched the houses for guns,
ransacking them in the process, the Attuans were allowed to return home.

There are conflicting accounts about what happened to Etta and Foster Jones,
and the death of Foster Jones is especially controversial. According to one Unangan
man, the Japanese knew Foster Jones had a radio and tortured him to find it, then
killed him. Japanese reports and some Attuans, including Nick Golodoff, have said
that Foster Jones killed himself or attempted to commit suicide. Several sources
agree that Etta Jones had wounds on her wrists but that they were not mortal.
According to some accounts, Foster Jones also slit his wrists. However, Mike
Lokanin, who was ordered to bury Jones, denied this story. When he told Mike
that Jones was dead, one of the Japanese soldiers pantomimed cutting his wrist
to indicate that Jones had killed himself. Mike, however, was skeptical and said
later that it was clear that Jones was deliberately killed. When Jones's body was
exhumed at Attu in 1948, examination confirmed that he had been shot through
the head (Kohlhoff 1995:42).

The next morning, the Native residents of the village were assembled at the
flagpole, and the Japanese flag was raised (Stein n.d.:9). Later some of the Attuans
covertly mocked the flag, calling it the "Japanese meatball" or saying it looked like
a target. One of them stole the American flag back and hid it from the Japanese.
The Japanese soldiers took some food from the Attuans, but their commander[13]
returned the stolen food. He ordered the Unangan residents to stay in their houses
and made the village off-limits to soldiers (Kohlhoff 1995:43). The Japanese
roped off the houses of the village, evidently more to discourage the Japanese soldiers from bothering or stealing from the Attuans than to keep the Attuans inside
(Carter 1994:40–41).

---

[13] Kohlhoff states that this was Commander Yamazaki, but John Cloe has corrected that
statement. Major Matsutoshi Hozumi was the senior Japanese commander on Attu at the
time the soldiers stole the food. Colonel Yasuyo Yamazaki was the commander in charge
of Japanese forces during the Battle of Attu (John Cloe, pers. comm., July 2, 2011).

The Japanese troops occupied Attu for three months before they took the Unangan residents to Japan. During that time there was a death in the village, the elderly John Artumonoff, a former chief (Jolis 1994:11; Murray 2005). The Attuans found it difficult to fish, hunt, or collect food because they had to get permission from the Japanese every time they went out in a boat. When they caught fish, the Japanese confiscated some for their own use. Because the Attuans were not allowed to go looking for firewood, they had to burn boards from their houses. One of the Japanese officers wrote in his diary that the Attuans loved to wear bright colors, and some wore berets. He noted that although alcohol was forbidden on Attu, the villagers enjoyed sake and beer when the Japanese soldiers offered it to them. The officer said the chief's son "Little Mike" [George Hodikoff?] accompanied them on mountain hikes and boat rides and often played the guitar and accordion for them (Stewart 1978:62–63). Some of the other children also befriended the Japanese during these weeks in the summer of 1942. Kiri Sugiyama, a military photographer, took several pictures of Attuan children.

Some of the most familiar pictures of the Attuans are the ones the Japanese took

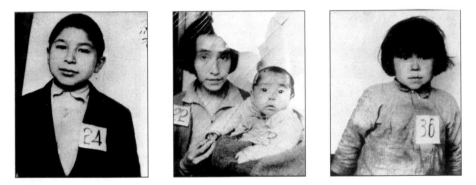

CLOCKWISE FROM TOP LEFT: Young boy, #24; Parascovia Lokanin and her baby, Tatiana, #22 and #23; Marina Hodikoff, #36; young man, #17; Elizabeth Prossoff, #8; Alex Prossoff, #31.
All images: Aleutian Pribilof Island Association

after pinning numbers to every man, woman, and child. These appear to have been taken in Attu, before the villagers were taken to Japan.

Mike Lokanin, 1947 (1988)[14]: In 1942, January 12th, I had a baby girl named Tatiana. We[15] stayed on Agattu all winter trapping foxes, and the boat was to take us off on February 15th or 19th. We were out of ammunition, flour, sugar, tea, and milk. We were completely out of everything. We were beginning to starve when finally M/S *Point Reyes* picked us up off Agattu. When we go in Attu, everything was blackout, and Mr. and Mrs. C. Foster Jones were in Attu. Mrs. Jones was the schoolteacher, and Mr. Jones was the radio man. There was plenty of snow in Attu then.

When I got in Attu I heard about war, war, but I never did see war, so I didn't care much, and I didn't think war would be at Alaska. Pretty soon I heard about Japanese are beginning to get near Alaska, but I still think Japs won't bother Attu because I know Attu is too small for them. We got word from the US government to pack up all our things. Sometime a boat will be in Attu to pick us up. So we already packed everything we got. Of course we got the things we need out so we can use it temporarily in the month of May. One day we see vessel come to outside of harbor, and it was rough. Wind was blowing from the northeast, and as soon as we saw the boat coming, we thought it was Japanese boat. After she got outside the harbor she wasn't anchored because wind was too rough for her to anchor out there, and she couldn't get inside the harbor.

Maybe about half an hour later we seen a launch coming into harbor. Some people still think it was Japanese boat. We look through scope. We can see letters on boat, " U.S.N.T." They had rough time coming in. Chief of Attu Mike Hodikoff and Second Chief Alfred Prokopeuff went down on beach to see if that's our transportation. Of course USN or USCG always visit Attu once or twice a year anyway, but people were talking about war. We got excited. When they come on beach, the officer got out and shake hands with both chiefs and the chief asks if this is our boat. Officer says he hasn't got word to pick anyone up off Attu. All they had was ten army troops with their supplies to be taken ashore on Attu, but the weather was too rough to take anything over the sea in small boats, so they said they were going to land them on Kiska Island if they can. Officer want Mike Hodikoff and Alfred to go on *Casco* for two or three days so they can show a good landing place in any kind of weather. They stayed out four days and came back.

---

[14] Mike Lokanin's firsthand account, published in Ethel Ross Oliver's 1988 book *Journal of an Aleutian Year*, was reproduced without editing. His account is edited here for readability.

[15] Just before this part of Lokanin's account, he says that in 1939 he married Parascovia Horisoff.

The whole community sent out ten pelts to Dutch Harbor for sale to navy because they didn't have a thing in store. All they got was flour, few cans salmon, corned beef. No sugar, no butter, no milk or coffee, so they got some food off the *Casco*. Mr. Fred Schroeder did not come back from San Francisco with supplies for store. Later, last part of May, a sub come to Attu, a patrolling sub. All the men were invited to the sub, and when we got to the submarine, the captain took all the men inside and show inside of sub to everyone. And then he got on deck and, laying against the rail on the side, he asked some questions about how often the Japs come around Attu a year in present time. I was standing back against cabin and talking to one of the crew, and I saw the captain was laying against the rail and the chain busted, and he went overboard in water and everyone on deck start to laugh. He fell backwards. When he reach the water he swim for the dory, which was ours, tied along the side of the sub. He couldn't pull himself in, so some men went down and help him in the dory. When he got on deck, he look at us and smile. He went below. A half hour later he come out and said he is ready to leave now. He told us as soon as we see Japs boat, please notify Dutch Harbor. We got off, and the sub took off, too. That's the only US boat we seen since 1942 to 1945, until at Okinawa when we got out of prison camp.

June we had nice all the way. Not much rain, not much wind, sunshine all the time. Of course, we were always standing by all the time for boat to pick us up.

One day we heard over the radio the Japs were bombing Dutch Harbor. We still hear war on radio. One day the Attu men were getting ready for going out to gather driftwood. They get their boats ready and fill up five-gallon can with gasoline and mix it with lube oil. Everything was ready for the next day. All over the village, everyone was in deep with a sad looking face. You can tell something is gon' happen, but they didn't know what is coming to them. I myself feel something strange going to happen to us.

One of the other men said when I visited his house that he got some kind of heart trouble. He said maybe too much blood pressure. I asked him what is trouble. Oh, he said, my heart keep bothering me. I cannot go to sleep, my heart is just like it comes up to my throat. If it does that I feel awful weakened. I asked him if he was going out for wood with the other men. He said, I don't feel like going, but anyways I got to go.

I myself didn't feel so good, but I didn't pay any attention to what I felt. Once in awhile I can feel my heart thump just like it choke me, but I don't pay any attention to it. Most everyone looked sad to me.

That day the village was so quiet, all I can hear is the gas motors of the power plant which runs three times a day by the school house. All we can hear is PUTT

PUTT PUTT—even the kids don't like to play. It was really nice at evening time. All the way out it was clear. The island seems to be sitting on top of the surface out in the ocean. When I look at the mountain, everything is green. Flowers are beginning to blossom. Things look awful nice. When I sniff in air I can smell flowers, and looking to the mountains on each side of village, they look clearer than I ever saw them before. Little fog string 'round foot of mountains looks nice. Hardly any breeze come from the southwest. Most of the houses are smoking. When I pass some houses, I smell the boiled salmon. At my house too, my wife is boiling salmon for supper. I went down to the other end of village to see what's doing, and I met John on the road. I asked him if he was going out with his father tomorrow. He told me he will be out tomorrow if the weather keeps like this. He say it will be lots of fun tomorrow going to get seagull eggs, and shooting ducks, and getting wood. He asked me why don't I come in his boat. I already got a boat to go anyway. Most of the fourteen-footers carry two men, and two or three five-gallon cans of gasoline, and guns, and cooking equipment. They don't have much room if they carry three men. I told him I already got to go in someone's boat. Now the sun was getting in back of the mountain and the shadow showed on the other side of the bay. When I looked toward the school, I see Mr. Foster Jones was coming out of his powerplant house, which is ten feet away from the school. He was oiling his motor. Of course he always run it at midnight, too. I kept walking around. There was no wind and the ocean in the bay was just like water in a pan on the table. When I look out the bay, I can see the seagulls and sea parrots flying, and little birds waving beside the old ravens flying over the village, and cawing. I never see so many crows in my life before as now, I thought to myself.

I stopped in Alfred's house. His wife is my aunt, and sometimes I go visit her house. I had few cups of tea with her. I visited my aunt's house until it was getting a little dark. When I start to my own house, which is fifty or sixty feet away, I can hear "chipee" birds still chirping and still seagulls calling. I got home.

When I got home, my wife had table ready and was waiting for me. My daughter was sleeping on the bed. My wife said things look very quiet, lonesome today. I had my supper and went to lay down on my bed and something in my mind tells me something is going to happen. One thing was steady in my mind: Japanese will be here tomorrow. But I couldn't figure it out.

My wife was sitting by me and said, "Darling, are you going out with the other men for wood?" I told her I'll be out tomorrow. "Bring some seagull eggs when you come home," she said, and I told her "I will if I can." I told my wife that I have a hunch Japs will be here sometime. She said to me, "I hope not, they might kill everyone." Every time when my heart thumps, it makes me feel sick and weak. It's about 11 p.m. so I told my wife I am going to bed now. She told me, "Darling, before you go to bed, get some water, there is no water in the house for morning." I got up and get water from my aunt's house. The sky was nice and clear. Then I go to bed. My wife was still up washing dishes. I didn't have to, that's why I go to sleep.

Innokenty Golodoff, 1966: Before the Japs came to Attu in 1942, the navy was going to take us away. The navy came out in May and left about ten men and 160 drums of gasoline, but they didn't take us away because it was too stormy. The Navy had ten guns, and they couldn't leave them all at Attu, so they took them to Kiska Harbor, and the Japs took them the same day they took Attu. The Japs came in on June 7, 1942, and took Attu, and I guess they used the navy's gasoline. The Japs didn't land near our village. They landed on the west side in Holtz Bay. At night we heard them coming in.

Some of us young men were going to fight the Japs. When we saw their ships coming, we got out our guns and all our bullets. Then one of the old men came and talked to us and told us not to fight. He said, "We are not enough to fight so many men."

Early in the morning, we saw the ship. We didn't know what kind of ship it was. About 11 a.m. after we had church—it was Sunday—the Japs came into the village. They came in over the point on the west side of Chichagof Harbor. I didn't know what to do, so I ran off to the hill on the east side and hid under rocks. I stayed there half a day and then I came back. I had nothing to eat. Six men stayed out all day. The Japs were looking for them but couldn't find them, so they sent some of the village men out to bring them in.

The first Japs that came into our village were young kids. They were pretty bad—they shot into the houses. They hit Annie Hoodikoff [Hodikoff] in the leg. The Jap doctor fixed her. She died in Tacoma hospital about 1946, after we got back from Japan. She had TB.

Right after the first bunch of Japs, the second bunch came. They were better. They were the officers and they made the young kids stop shooting.

Alex Prossoff, 1947 (1988)[16]: We were having church services in the little Russian church in Attu on Sunday morning, June 7, 1942, when boats entered the harbor. When the gunboats got closer to the village, we saw that they were Japs.

---

[16] Alex Prossoff's firsthand account, published in Ethel Ross Oliver's 1988 book *Journal of an Aleutian Year*, was reproduced without editing. His account is edited here for readability.

They started machine-gun fire on the village. Some of our boys ran for their rifles to fight the Japs, but Mike Hodikoff, our chief, said, "Do not shoot, maybe the Americans can save us yet."

Mike Lokanin, 1947 (1988): June 7th, '42, Sunday in the morning, early when I was sleeping, someone was knocking at my door, so I got up and look who it was. He said, "I am Fred" with a frightened voice. I was wondering what was the matter, so I ask him what was the matter. He told me there is boats out there, and they are unknown boats, don't have any flag on either. One big, two-chimneyed boat. It might be Japs.

I ask how many there are. He was half frightened and shaking. He said he don't know, it looks like more than four or five. So then he got out and went down to his house, and I went to my bed again. It was 3:00 a.m. It was too early for me to get up anyway. My wife was awake too. She asked me what was the matter and who was at the door. I told her it was Fred, and she start to nurse her baby. I went back to sleep again. I usually get up at 7:00 a.m. and build a fire and make breakfast, eat with my wife. I was just about to get up when someone was at my door again. I got out of my bed and look out through the window. It is Fred again. I said to him what's the trouble, Fred? He said the boats look like Japanese boats. I said to him why, if it's Japanese they could come right in the harbor and shoot the village. I said to him why don't he go to the school and tell Mr. Jones about it and maybe he can send a wire to Dutch Harbor.

I'm beginning to think it might be Japs too. I go in my house and Fred left. I said to my wife, "Honey, Fred said Japanese boats outside the harbor." She lift her head off her pillow, look at her baby, and said "Oh God bless us, what we'll do then?" I said to her, "nothing we can do, honey, God knows what we'll do and if our time is come, we'll be dead. If our hour is there, we'll be dead. So all we can do is think of God in our heart; that is all."

She said, "Oh my dear little baby." She got tears in her eyes as she spoke. I told her I am going out and see what the others are doing. When I got out of my house and start to my aunt's house, I saw a little skiff was going out to Cannon Island to get a close look at the boats. When I got to my aunt's house, most of the village men were lined up alongside of the house and they all were talking and talking. Trying to figure out what kind of boats they are, what nationality. We saw a plane flying, circling around, but it didn't seem to bother anything at all. The third time he come to circle around, he got close. We saw the red ball on the wings and on each side of the plane. It was a single motor and two-winged and had two men, one in back of the pilot. He was the gunner. He had machine guns on each side of him.

It was about 8:30 a.m. Everyone was getting ready for church. That was their last time forever entering their church. Before church, my brother-in-law Aleck and another person who went out in a skiff came ashore. They all said it is Japanese boats. We went to school to talk to Mr. C. Foster Jones and told him the Japs' boats are outside the harbor, and we ask him to send message to Dutch Harbor because he got words to say to the US government when he sees Japs or if we see Japs and tell him. He is supposed to say, "the boys were out today and didn't see a boat and they came home and they are going to have a fried codfish." That means that Japanese boats have come here. We ask him to send message. He said it might be US marines or navy. He was sending weather reports to Dutch Harbor and I told him he might as well send a message because the boys have seen Japanese plane. He said if he make mistake and call up Dutch Harbor, it will be on his neck. So I just walk out.

I see Mrs. Jones curling her hair. I stop by her room and told her I am afraid they are Japs. She smile and said to me, "Oh it might be navy. If they are Japs, why, they could have been in long time ago." I just walk out.

I heard the church bell still ring. I did not go to church. Four of us went out to the point. The boat was so close we could see men walking on deck. Around twenty or twenty-five small landing barges went back and forth from Holtz Bay to the transport. We were walking along the edge of the hills, and the plane was flying 'round. Didn't seem to bother us, so we four of us thought it might be Americans too. So we just keep on walking to the edge of the hill and wave at the boat. It was nice and clear sunshine. I thought I heard a sound of talking. I told the others, "Hey, listen." I stood there and looked around. Finally I see men coming from back of the mountain on foot. One of the boys I was with told me, "let's go to them, they might be Americans." I told him I don't want to go to them, and we stood and watched them running and crawling on the ground. We look at boats, and boats are raising red and white flags and moving farther out in the ocean. We all made a run toward the village to see what will happen. We see men running down the mountain and hills. As soon as they reach the beach and cross the creek, they open machine gun and rifle fire at the village. I thought to myself, my wife and daughter are goners now. I thought in my mind, "It will be all right if they are killed without torture and suffering." The way the rifle and machine guns took off, we four of us thought nothing was left in the village. All we can see is men walking in the village, but they were the men who came to the village. We see Japs running to the village with guns in their hands. The first building they get in is the school where Mr. and Mrs. Foster Jones is. We thought Foster might send message to Dutch Harbor.

I told the boys, it's no use for us to go to the village now, the way the rifles and machine guns are shooting. Let's hide for the night and sneak up to the village at night and see if anything is left. So we crawl under a big rock which could weigh a thousand pounds. We heard a plane flying over us and we were going to take a peek at it and just about stuck our heads out when the big guns went off. Boy, we went back in under the rock; we were piled on top of each other. We stayed there almost the whole morning and afternoon.

In late afternoon we heard somebody was talking, and it was sound like one of our men. We said to each other, they might be hiding too. Suddenly I heard them calling us but I didn't answer because I want to make sure it's our men. By God, I could hear Willie and Fred's voices, so I pulled my head out and answered them, and I got out from under the rock with the rest of the boys. We looked around but we couldn't see anyone. I answered and said, "Who is that? Call us, please show up if you are there." I see someone sitting on a hill. It was Willie and Fred, which the Japs sent to look for us. We all come out from under the rock and we start to go home. We asked what was going on. Willie said in a low tone, them little Japs got us now. Fred said, we were afraid of Japs before, now we got to be afraid of Americans. Fred turned his head around with his mad-looking face and said, "We all under Japs instead of Americans." I asked him if anyone got killed. He said everyone was okay except his wife got hit in her leg, but the Japanese doctor fix her. I asked him, how is my wife and kid? He said they are all okay. I would like to ask more, but he looked awful mad, and I was kind of afraid to ask him. I told him, let's go now. Willie told me they had been looking for me all over the place and couldn't find me or the boys with me. Also one boy was missing, Sergie Artumonoff. On the way home we find him, he give up because he seen us walking all together. When he walk up to us he said, aren't the Japs going to hurt me? We told him, oh Japs won't do any hurt to you. He began to smile.

Fred told me I got to go to the school. So when we got to the school, I walk in. All the doors have got Japanese guards. In the schoolroom I see Mr. and Mrs. C. Foster Jones sitting on one of the school desks. I said hello to Mr. Jones but one of the guards said to me, "No no, no talk to Amelika." He was trying to tell me not to talk with the American. Foster said to me anyway, "Well, Mike, the world has seemed to change today. We are under Japanese rule now." I was going to tell him it was his fault, too, but I thought it was too late now. I just looked at him without saying a word. Just then the Japanese MP came in with the American flag under his arm. He came to me and started to read a paper, which was a proclamation. Of course he read in his language. He's got an interpreter with him. The MP stands in front of me and reads the paper. I couldn't understand the words. The interpreter explains the meaning of the words, that the Japanese capture us from the US government. Now we are under the Japanese government. Japanese government will keep us under one condition: that from now on, we must obey the Japanese. After reading the proclamation he told me to go home and not to go around unless I get permission from Commander Yamadaki [Yamazaki?].

So I went home and my house was in bad-looking shape. Everything was thrown on the floor. My door was spoiled, eight bullet holes on the end of the house, two bullet holes in my stove, one going through to the fireplace, and my wife wasn't home. All my guns are gone and some other things were gone. I didn't care much about the guns. I hated to lose my watch with twenty-one jewels. All my papers were scattered on the floor. So I went down to the chief's house, my wife usually stays there if I am not home. By golly she was there. I walk in and look for my daughter. I didn't see her so I ask my wife, where is Taty. She was sleeping.

My wife was serving tea, and she ask me if I like to have cup of tea. I sure need it too. I told her yes. She gave me a cup, and I was just about going to drink my tea and one Jap came in. They were looking for me, he said. I just left the table and go out with him.

He told me to help Mr. Jones move out of the school, so I went in there.

Fellow named Kasukabe, interpreter, was in the school, and Mr. and Mrs. Jones were picking up their things. The man had a sword. Mr. Jones had a big load under his arm. This Jap wanted him to take some more. He said, Alec and Mike will take them to me. The Jap said, "No you take them," and he slapped Mr. Jones on his face and knocked him down on floor and start to kick him on the body, and picked him up and slapped him down again, and kicked him out the door. But they didn't touch Mrs. Jones, and they didn't touch Alec and me. After he kicked Mr. Jones out, he pulled his sword out of its case and went after Mr. Jones. Of course I couldn't see what happened after he kicked him out. Anyway, I was so scared I was shaking. Seems like I am going to shake the whole village down. I was trying to brace myself, but I was still shaking. The Japs take Mr. and Mrs. Jones to the trader's house. Of course the trader, which is Mr. Fred Schroeder, is not on Attu. Lucky he's not on Attu; if he was, he might be dead or taken to Japan too.

On the way I find Mrs. Jones' slipper stuck in the dirt. Soon as I deliver the things in there to them, I just come to my house and I stayed outside trying to cool myself from shaking. I didn't want to scare my wife. I walked into my house, and my wife looked at me. She said, "What's the matter, Honey, you look pale." "Oh," I said. "I just don't feel good, maybe from catching cold."

You better warm up Honey, she said. She had a little supper ready. We didn't have much left in the house. Sugar was gone and milk also. I had to bum milk from

Elizabeth Prossoff for my baby. After I got eaten my supper, I helped Pari cleaning dishes, and I told her what happened to Mr. and Mrs. Jones. She said to me, "Honey they might do the same thing to us." I told her I don't think so. After we finish dishes it is past 12 a.m. Day started to break about 1:30 a.m. I went to bed with my wife. I couldn't go to sleep. I rolled in my bed. It was light and bright too. Boy, the machine guns go off in the air, and I heard plane. I went out on my porch, and I see the plane was flying very low. It made a turn and goes out over the point without any bullet touching. I lit a fire in the stove, and when I had coffee ready, called my wife. She wasn't sleeping. She got up and had coffee with me. She said to me, "Honey, what plane was the Japanese shooting at?" I said to her it was American plane. She said to me, "God bless, they might bomb this place."

As I was talking with my wife, I heard someone come. I looked out. It was Kasukabi [or Kasukabe], the fellow who kicked Mr. Jones last night. The Jap was in hurry too. I was wondering what was going on. He comes to my door and calls me. I went out. He said good morning, and I said good morning to him.

Mr. Foster Jones is dead. Of course I didn't ask him how he died. They had two interpreters. One was named Imai, a young fellow, and the other was Kasukabi. He was higher; he had three stars. Mr. Imai had only two stars on his collar. When I get down near Schroeder's house, I met Mr. Imai for the first time.

He said to me, "Are you interpreter too?" Looks to me he is nice to talk with. I asked him how Foster died. He said he don't know it either. Later Mr. Kasukabe come to us and he started to talk. He was talking in his language; I couldn't understand what he said. I see him cut across his wrist with his finger. Someone came out and called him. He goes in the house, and Imai looked around before he spoke to me. Then he said Foster cut his own wrist with his pocketknife. I was thinking, after they capture Foster Jones I don't see why they left his pocketknife for him.

They called us in. He was half sunk in his own blood. They won't let me see his face or body. He was wrapped in a blanket. They told me to bury him without a coffin. So I dug a grave by our church. I measured the distance from the corner of the church with my eyes and tried to remember the wind direction. He was buried in the southwest corner of the church. The grave depth was seven feet, and distance from church to grave fifteen feet. After I buried him that was end of him then, and I tried never to forget where I buried his body. And Imai was by me all the time I work.

Some of us Attuans stay by Mrs. Jones all the time. We don't know what the Japs might do to her.... Mr. Kasukabe lost one star. Mr. Imai received three stars. He got higher after Foster got murdered.

Alex Prossoff, 1947 (1988): A few of the boys ran away. Japs landed and came running into the village, shooting. Lucky only one woman get hurt. She is shot in leg. So much shooting and machine gun bullets flying all around, Japs kill some of their own men. They capture the village. Some Japs take Mr. and Mrs. Jones and all the Natives to schoolhouse and keep us there whole day without food and water. Mr. Jones is radio man. Mrs. Jones is schoolteacher. They very nice people. The Japs keep us there until nine o'clock at night. The Joneses live in schoolhouse, but the Japs want the building, so they tell them to leave. Mr. Jones try to take little food. The Japs beat and kicked them. They knocked them down. Some of us take a few of their things over to Mr. Schroeder's house, and then we could not do anything more for them, and the Japs let us go home.

Next morning the Japs tell us Foster Jones is dead. Mike Lokanin buried him by the church. He was just wrapped in blanket. Mike said his wrists are cut. We tried to make Mrs. Jones comfortable. Some of us stay with her all the time. She is sick and has bad cuts on her wrists, too. But she gets well.

Japs have taken down our flag, but Innokinty gets it and hides it. I hide the church money. The Japs go through our houses and take many things until one officer stop them. They put lines around our houses, and Jap soldiers are not allowed to bother us.

Olean Prokopeuff (Golodoff), 1981: The year 1942, on a Sunday morning, the Japanese armed forces came and captured us. They came from the interior of our island after daybreak. That morning, a Japanese airplane flew around the village three times. The teacher [Etta Jones] was informed of this by the villagers. Instead of informing the authorities, the teacher told the villagers that there were lots of American patrol planes patrolling this area. After the teacher told them that, the villagers felt secure. After they came down from the hills, it was said that our village was surrounded by them.

After that, the villagers went up to the observation hill and saw the Japanese fleet anchored in the bay on the other side. As they were attacking in force, one of our ladies was shot in her leg. As they were firing their weapons in all directions during their assault, their forces also hit their own men, and it is believed that a few of their own men had been killed.

After they came, they went to Alfred's wife's house. Since my house was being shot at, and since I was being scared, I went to Alfred's wife's house carrying my three year child, Elizabeth.

From there we went to Alfred's wife's house, where she was lying in bed with a sore leg. After we went to Alfred's wife's house, the Japanese soldiers surrounded it. They faced the house and had their rifles aimed at it. So at that point in time, Perocoviya [Parascovia] sat down. I then thought to myself, "What if I get shot standing up? I would drop the child and she might hurt herself." So I, too, sat down. The Japanese soldiers did not shoot, and an officer got there in time to give orders to move away from the house. So the soldiers moved. The Japanese had an interpreter who spoke English pretty well. He told us to follow him to the schoolhouse, and we followed him there.

After we arrived at the school, when a fire was made outside, I was afraid that the schoolhouse was going to be set afire with all of us in there. Since we weren't being set on fire, we were asked if we were all present. We stated that three of our young men were out. They waited for the young men to come back to the village but there was no sign of them. The young men did not return from hiding until some of the village men went out and escorted them back to the village. Only then did they return.

The young men were brought home then we were sent back to our houses. When we went into our homes, everything was scattered on our floors, even the Easter eggs were on the floor. It was never determined what the Japanese searched for.

We all stayed inside our homes. The guards stayed by our homes with bayonets. They were standing around guarding like that for three days. Once daybreak came, some flares were shot into the air. We went under our beds because of being scared, not knowing what was happening.

Innokenty Golodoff, 1966: We lived on Attu three months after the Japs came. They guarded our houses all the time. We could go outside for fresh air but not away from the houses, except that they let us go out and fish once in a while. We had to eat our own food. We didn't have to give the Japs any food. They didn't bother our women.

Alex Prossoff, 1947 (1988): More and more Japs come to Attu. Many of their men get sick. They make their camp all around our village. They pile their things on the beach. One time I tell them wrong thing, and storm comes and they lose lots of their things. They get very mad and tell me next time I tell them wrong thing, they kill me.

All summer long the Japs stayed on Attu. We did not have much food, but sometimes they would let us go out in dory to fish. They made us take little Jap flag on our boat. We used to make fun of it and say it looks like target. We cannot hunt wood, so we have to tear boards from inside our homes to burn.

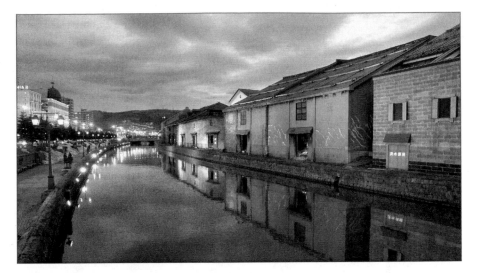

Otaru Canal, March 25, 2008. *http://commons.wikimedia.org/wiki/File:Otaru_Hokkaido_Japan.jpg*

Life as a Japanese POW

The Attuans boarded a merchant ship, the *Yoko Maru*, in mid-September of 1942. The Japanese soldiers allowed them to bring food, blankets, and even furniture with them, perhaps with the idea that their move to Japan might be permanent. The village was standing when they left, but US forces destroyed it in subsequent air and sea raids, as well as in the Battle of Attu.[17]

The trip to Japan began September 14 and took about two weeks. Alfred Prokopeuff's and Elizabeth Prossoff's mother, Anecia Prokopeuff, died onboard ship between Attu and Kiska, and she was buried at sea (Carter 1994:46). At Kiska the Attuans were transferred to another ship, the *Nagata Maru*.[18] Their quarters were in a cargo hold that had been used to carry coal. They had to stay in the hold except for daily periods on deck (Kohlhoff 1995:85-86).

---

[17] After the boat carrying the Attuans left the island in September 1942, some Japanese troops stayed on Attu, in Massacre Bay. The next year, in May 1943, the Americans retook the island of Attu in a bloody battle that resulted in some 550 American and 2,350 Japanese deaths. In the final battle, about 700 Japanese died in a desperate, last-ditch charge. The Japanese survivors committed suicide, except for a few who were taken prisoner (John Cloe, pers. comm.).

[18] The boat was identified by Gengoro S. Toda of Japan, a user of the Tully's Port website (http://propnturret.com/tully), a listserve devoted to Japanese military vessels. Another Tully's Port user, "Bob," [Bob Hackett], found information indicating that the gunboat *Nagata Maru* brought construction materials and food from Yokosuka, Japan, to Attu, arriving August 27, 1942. After transporting troops between Kiska and Attu, she departed Kiska on September 17, 1942 and arrived in Otaru, Hokkaido, on September 27, 1942.

The ship finally arrived at the Japanese city of Otaru, on the west side of Hokkaido Island, at the end of September. The passengers were very dirty from the coal dust and had not bathed since they left Attu (Carter 1994:46). Their first house was a vacant railroad employee dormitory on Wakatake-cho. They stayed on the second floor in four rooms, each about 142 square feet. The furniture and belongings they had brought were stored at the rear of the dormitory (Stewart 2008:302–303).

It must have been a big culture shock for the Attuans to come to live in an industrial city. Otaru's population in 1940 was about 164,000, somewhat larger than its 2008 population of about 138,000. The city is in Ainu territory, but the Ainu had been decimated by disease several centuries earlier. Today, Otaru is a tourist destination for Japanese and Russians.

Mr. Kawashima, one of the Japanese soldiers who had occupied the village, visited the Attuans in Otaru in late 1942 or early 1943. He said that two of the boys, "Ivan" [probably John Golodoff] and his younger brother Nick, hugged him in greeting, and that Ivan told him their sister Helen had already died (Stewart 1978:28).

There are differing reports of the Attuans' diet in Otaru. In August 1942, a Japanese soldier who visited them saw that they had bread, rice, meat, and vegetables. He thought they were eating better than most Japanese (Stewart 2008:303). At that point, the Unangan probably still had food they had brought with them from Attu. Innokenty Golodoff remembered that at first the food was only slightly meager—rice, bread, and a little fish and pickled radishes (Golodoff 1966:8–9).

In addition to not having enough to eat, many of the Attuans were weakened by other medical circumstances, particularly tuberculosis. Several of them died of that disease in Japan. Dr. Satoru Nogushi examined the Attuans soon after they arrived in Otaru and found that about half of them were suffering from acute tuberculosis. He thought their conditions were exacerbated by their meager diet on Otaru, which lacked protein and calories (Stewart 2008:303). Several died from beriberi, a disease of malnutrition. This may have been caused by a diet almost entirely made up of white rice. Mike Hodikoff and his son both died of food poisoning in 1945 from eating rotten garbage (Kohlhoff 1995:132).

The Attu residents worked digging dolomite, a kind of clay, from an open pit while they were there. Nick remembers going with his mother to the clay mine and waiting for her while she worked. According to Innokenty Golodoff, the Attuans didn't work very hard. Although they were supposed to be paid between one-half and one yen per day, they were not paid at the time. When they were released, those who had worked were given about seven hundred dollars in yen to take back to the United States. Unfortunately, this money was collected by US officials and the equivalent in American money never given to the workers. The Unangan worked only during the first part of their internment, and even then, on most days only a few of them worked. The voluntary labor of Aleuts contrasted sharply with the treatment of Chinese and Korean prisoners, who were marched to work every day (Stewart 2008:303).

In 1944, the twenty-nine (of the original forty) Attuans still living were moved from the Wakatake-cho dormitory to a larger house at Shimizu-cho, which had previously served as clergy quarters for a Shinto shrine. Partitions divided the families (Stewart 2008:302-303). The Attuans' new home was farther from the clay pits, and they didn't work after that. Their declining health may have also prevented them from working.

After the Japanese surrendered, the Attuans were able to walk more freely around the city of Otaru. Alex Prossoff even remembered that they met a Russian couple named Soffieff and attended Russian Orthodox Church services (Prossoff 1988). In 1942, a count of foreign nationals in Japan found forty-eight Old Russian residents living in Hokkaido (Foreign Resident Population 2011). Contrary to most reports, Stewart found that the Attuans were allowed much freedom of movement in Otaru throughout their stay in the city. According to him, the children frequented the candy store, and the adults bought food at the butcher and fish shops (Stewart 2008:302–303). It is unlikely, however, that they had money to make such purchases, which also contradict the malnutrition and starvation of the Attuans.

Communication between the Attuans and the Japanese was in English, while the Attuans spoke Unangam Tunuu (Aleut) among themselves. Nick Golodoff remembered that the Japanese often wrote notes in English to convey their orders or questions. On Attu, Angelina Hodikoff served for a time as an interpreter, translating the Japanese soldiers' English into Unangam Tunuu (Jolis 1994:16). In Japan, the Unangan were expected to learn Japanese (Stewart 2008:303). A Japanese linguist, Ken Hattori, visited them in 1943 and recorded and made notes on their language.

Innokenty Golodoff said that at first the Japanese were pretty rough, but later they got friendlier. The Unangan internees remembered beatings and other mistreatment by guards. Julia Golodoff went for three days without food and water and had to shovel snow in her bare feet as punishment for shouting at one of the guards about her daughter's death. Japanese sources, too, acknowledge that the Attuans were sometimes victims of violence at the hands of their guards (Stewart 2008:303).

At least one of their captors became their friend, however: Mr. Shikanai, the policeman who lived with them in both of their houses in Otaru. On Christmas Eve in 1944, Shikanai obtained goat meat and turkey for a party, and the Unangan played the accordion and danced into the night (Kohlhoff 1995:133). After the war was over, when an American army plane came to take the Attuans back to the United States, they had a sake drinking party with Shikanai (Golodoff 1966:9).

The main hardship of internment in Japan was the lack of healthful food. After their own food was gone, the Attuans began to starve and suffer from malnutrition. They rarely got any fruits or vegetables, only a small ration of rice. They could see that their Japanese guards were hungry too (Golodoff 1966:9).

Forty people came to Otaru, but only twenty-four left. Twenty-one people died, including four of the five babies born while they were in Japan.

Olean Prokopeuff (Golodoff), 1981: After three days, we were taken aboard a ship, and we were on our way. My house was opened and burned. We were taken out to the ship when it was getting dark. After spending the night on board the ship with much whistling and running about going on, and because of our ignorance of exactly what was happening, we were very anxious. Later on we were told that an American submarine was detected and that was the cause for all the commotion. A shortcut was said to be taken to where they were going. (I was not aware of what shortcut they meant.) After traveling for some time, we were told that we were passing by a navy yard. All during the voyage, we were kept in a hold which was very unpleasant smelling, and it was also dark. We never once saw daylight until we reached Japan.

Innokenty Golodoff, 1966: When the Japs were ready to leave in September, they carried all our stuff onto their ships for us. We took our blankets, beds, chairs—everything except our houses. The Japs treated us pretty good. Two of them spoke English. None of us were scared when they took us on the ship—no women cried. Then we went to Kiska and went to another ship—a bigger one. We stayed at Kiska for one day.

Mike Lokanin, 1947 (1988): From the 7th of June to the 1st of September, 1942, we had been told to be ready to go to Japan. So we got everything ready. Imai tells us we better take as much food to Japan as we can. It is hard to get food in Japan maybe. So each family takes flour, sugar, barrels of salt fish. We don't know how we are going to live in Japan, so we take tents, stoves, fish nets, windows, and doors also. Good thing we did. One day, 14 September 1942, a coal carrier came and they told us to get ready, we're going to Japan. We take our stuff to the vessel.

We got aboard late, past midnight. They put us down in the hold where the coal had been. Everything was all black and dirty. Some of the little kids didn't want to leave Attu. They cried, but the Jap soldiers picked them up and threw them down in the hold too. There are forty-two of us Attu people and Mrs. Jones.[19] Some old people are scared very bad. The vessel starts off for Kiska, and one of our people died on the boat. It was Alfred Prokopeuff's mother and the captain told us to throw her overboard. So we let her go overboard in between Kiska and Attu Pass. Next morning when we got to Kiska, there were plenty of Japs there, as in Attu. Some houses are bombed.

Three submarines were there. Three sunken boats were there too, and about twelve destroyers were there. Another vessel was a big army transport. That was the one that would to take us to Japan. Everybody was kind of afraid because if an American sub or plane comes, it will be our end. That evening we take off for Japan. On the way to Japan we were kept in the hatch and not allowed to come outdoors.

Olean Prokopeuff (Golodoff), 1981: When we reached Japan, the captain collided with the dock, and when this happened, we were thrown from our seated position right onto the deck. Then we thought to ourselves, "Ayayaa! Did our ship get shot?" This was a scary experience.

Finally, we were gathered on top of the dock. Then we were sprayed. Later on, we were picked up by a vehicle and taken to a black house. Since we fed ourselves with our own food from home during the trip, the only different food that was given to us was some warm rice. It was the only warm food we ate.

When asked if we were hungry, we told them yes. A meal was cooked for us that day. They brought our food on a tray. Chopsticks, which we did not know how to use, were given to us to use. There was a policeman present there with his partner. So as soon as they started talking with each other and not paying attention to us, we would quickly eat with our hands. When the policeman turned towards us, we would pretend like nothing had happened at all. We were also served an unusual-looking cooked bird with its feathers still on it. We felt suspicious of the cooked bird and so we did not eat it. After we were fed, we were put to bed.

Alex Prossoff, 1947 (1988): Then one day in September, a coal carrier came and they told us to get ready, we are going to Japan. One Japanese man who was kind to us tell us we better take as much food with us as we can, for it is hard to get food in Japan, maybe. So we do. Each family takes flour, sugar, and barrels of salt fish.

---

[19] According to Etta Jones, she was separated from the Attuans and taken to Yokohama before the Attuans went in a different boat to Hokkaido (Breu 2009:180).

We are all put down in hold of coal carrier where coal had been. Everything all black and dirty. Some of the little children do not want to leave Attu. They cry, but Japs soldiers pick them up and throw them down in holds, too. There are forty-two of us, old men and women, young people and the children. Most all the women and older girls going to have babies.

First we go to Kiska. A white man, Mr. House, is with us here. He was navy man on Kiska when Japs take it. There were ten American navy men there. The Japs take all of them prisoners, but Mr. House runs away and hides from Japs. He eats things he finds, plants and pootchky and along the beach. But finally, he can't find anything more because he doesn't know. So he goes to the Japs and gives up. We never see him after we get to Japan.

My wife's mother gets sick on the coal carrier and died. They make us just throw her into the sea. We could go on deck once a day for fresh air, but if we were going by any cities we had to stay in the hold.

After thirteen or fourteen days, one night, about 11:00 p.m., we landed at the city of Otaru on the island of Hokkaido in Japan. We stayed onboard the ship until daylight. When morning came some Japs soldiers, some policemen, and some Japs doctors came on board. They examined all of us but did not find any disease. They took us ashore then; we do not see Mrs. Jones again.

I was just wondering where they will take us when they brought us to a house that looked like nobody had lived in it for very long time, fifteen or ten years. It was very dirty, but even then, Japs make us take off our shoes before we can go in.

They ask us all kinds of questions about American. They asked me if Americans are good people, if we have any military outposts on our island, if we know where there were outposts in the Aleutian Islands, how often the coast guard and American warships came into Attu harbor. One of our head men told us not to tell the truth to them, so we did not tell them the right things. They asked us how many white people lived with us, and we told them just two, the teacher and the radio man. I told them the Japs killed the man. They asked us which army we liked best, Japs or Americans. Mike and I are only ones who talk to them. I tell them I can understand American language and that they are very kind to us. As long as Americans are fight for my country I'll be on their side. I told them Japs destroy our homes, make us prisoners, and put us on a land where we cannot talk his language. So I cannot say Japs are good people.

All of us are kept in one house. There are forty-two of us in one five-room house. We put our mattresses and blankets on the floor to sleep on. It was getting winter, and we did not have enough blankets to keep warm. We had only one stove we brought with us from Attu. The women cooked for all of us on it. The Japs did give us little heaters, but we did not have enough coal to keep us warm. They give us only one bucket of coal for all day.

Olean Prokopeuff (Golodoff), 1981: Our mattresses were laid on the floor. Pillows were also given to us, and they were very hard, but we did not complain. The blankets that were given to us were almost as thick as the mattresses, but we used them anyway. Every morning the floor was mopped. The house that we were staying at had a kitchen downstairs. We had a stove that we had taken from Attu which we used there.

We had soup that looked like grass and some dried rice. When we ran out of grass soup, we started making rice soup. Prior to this, we ate the food that we brought along from Attu, like the dried fish, the salted fish, and so on, but when we ran out of food, we were given vegetables like carrots, potatoes, and so on. After eating the boiled potatoes, we would have very bad stomachaches, and they were very painful.

It so happened one day that we were told that some officials were coming there to our place for a visit. A Japanese cook was brought there for us. They told us not to go away, and the Japanese cook put wood into the oven. He lit it, and as a result of that, the smoke filled the room. I can't remember whether or not cooking took place that day.

We were once again grouped and questions were asked of us. They asked if we were eating good food. We did not give them any reply. They once again asked us if we wanted to talk. We refused to talk. Then after that, we were given food once more.

Innokenty Golodoff, 1966: When we got to Japan, we landed at Otaru on the west side of Hokkaido. We went to the town—or city I guess—it was kind of big. They put us in one house—a big wooden house. Two policemen lived there with us. They gave us rice, and bread, and some fish once in awhile, and a little bit of pickled radishes. A girlfriend, Kasha San, saved my life. She was a nurse, and she was good to me. She gave me extra rice and she brought me eggs. She talked a little bit of English. She was there for about a year then she went away. Then I didn't get any extra food.

Alex Prossoff, 1947 (1988): We were hungry, too. At first we did all right because we ate the flour and sugar and fish we brought from Attu. The Japs gave us only two cups of rice for about ten people a day. When our food was gone, we could not buy any more from Japs. Then we began to get very hungry.

Innokenty Golodoff, 1966: While we were at Otaru for about three years, we worked digging clay. We worked about eight hours a day. We didn't work very hard. We dug it off the top of the ground and took it to the factory in a wheelbarrow. The clay was white. I guess they made dishes out of it. Our policeman took us up in the morning—we walked—and then he came for us in the afternoon. For lunch we ate the rice we brought with us in a little tin box. We had our own spoon—I never learned to use chopsticks. We never heard any news about the war. We had electric lights. At night we talked or patched up our clothes. We didn't have anything to read.

Olean Prokopeuff (Golodoff), 1981: That land where we were was very hot. We worked with picks and shovels, shoveling away at the clay. Then the clay was dried and crushed. The clay was also being worked on in the factories during winter. While working on this clay, a particle of it went in my right eye. I was afraid that I was going to lose my eyesight, but I have managed to arrive here (on Atka) without having to wear glasses.

Alex Prossoff, 1947 (1988): A month after we get to Japan, we had to go to work for Japs. I dug clay for a week, and then I went to work in the clay factory. It was hard work. We worked from seven in the morning to five at night and got one day of rest in two weeks. The women, most of them were put to work, too.

Olean Prokopeuff (Golodoff), 1981: As things were, our men were put to work. Shortly after that, they started admitting our people to the hospital. The people were getting sick one after the other until I was almost the only one left at home to cook. While I was doing that, they took my husband to the hospital. After they took my husband, my children were starving. So when I went to fetch some water, I would pick orange peelings off the ground. Then I would cook them on the top of the heater. Then I fed them to my children, and only then would they stop crying for a while.

Shortly thereafter, they admitted my children to the hospital. They asked me to come to the hospital. So I went there and "Ayayaa!" The people that were admitted to the hospital were very sick. That day a few went home. Being unable to hear what was happening, I begged to be returned to work. So they started me working on clay....

Later on, those who were sent home from the hospital took ill again. They were taken once more to the hospital. We were allowed to visit the hospital for check-ups. Whenever they did that, I would ask my people what they were doing to them. They replied, "We are being inoculated." Ayayaa! We did not know what was being done to them.

But then the people were dying. Lots of people died there. My daughter and son were among those who were in the hospital. They would say, "Mother, come here and scratch me." So I would go over to him/her and, not knowing exactly where they wanted me to scratch, I would scratch then moved away from them. The reason why they were unable to specify where they wanted to be scratched was because they could not move.

When my husband was close to death, he sent for me. I went to the hospital, and he gave me some cigarettes which he had stashed away. Then I stayed awake with him most of the night. Then he told me if I were sleepy to go to sleep. So I went to sleep, and during my slumber, he died.

When I was awakened, I got up, and I noticed that in our religious custom when a person dies, he is not dressed, but I watched them dress him. After he was dressed, he was taken out. I did not know what they did to him. It was not until my Leonty died that I went to where they must have taken him. Leonty was put in an oven, and I was told to light some flowers, so I did. Then I went to the other room. After that, they pulled him out, and I did not like what I saw. I approached a Japanese priest and asked him if it was a sin to do that. He told me that the reason why they did that was because they did not have any burying space. They said that they hardly had any space for burying people.

Alex Prossoff, 1947 (1988): We lost twenty-one people in Japan. My stepmother gets sick first. She got TB, and Japs take her to kind of hospital. But there is no heat and very little food, so she died. Some died of beriberi. Our chief, Mike Hodikoff, and his son, George, eat from garbage can and get poison food. Lots of children and babies die because they hungry and nothing but rice.

Innokenty Golodoff, 1966: When the Japs came to Attu, we were forty-two people, and after the schoolteacher died, forty-one left Attu. But many Attu people died in Japan. They died of starving I guess. Only twenty-five people came back from Japan. The ones who didn't come back ate the rice for about two years, then they couldn't eat it anymore. They were sick and they couldn't, and the Japs didn't have anything else to give them. We never had any fruit or vegetables. I don't know if our policemen had any other food—all I ever saw them eat was rice. We had both white and brown rice.

My two brothers and one sister died in Japan. They never buried them—they burned them. They gave the bones and ashes back to us, and now they are buried at Atka. They sent them back after we got to Atka.

Alex Prossoff, 1947 (1988): One of the hardest things was we could not bury our dead. There are no burials in Japan. All are burned. When our people died they were burned, too, and the Japs gave us little boxes to put the bones in. This was hard to have to pick up the bones of our loved ones. We kept all our boxes carefully because we wanted to take them home to be buried someday.

I noticed that when a Jap body was burned, the bones did not fill the box, but when an Aleut was burned, the box was not big enough to hold what was left. I told a Jap guard that his people have small frames, much smaller than Attu people. Must be because his people eat too much rice.

When we first get to Japan, Japanese seem to have enough food, but later lots of Japs hungry, too. We never saw any Red Cross packages of food or clothing while we were in prison. No medicine ever came either. By 1944, we got so hungry we would dig in the hog boxes when the guards were not looking. Whatever we found, we would wash it, and cook it, and try to eat it. When spring came, we would work after five o'clock in some of the Jap gardens nearby for a little extra food. In summer, we sometimes helped the herring fishermen. One time I went fishing in the bay to show the Jap fishermen how we fish in Attu. All I caught was old boot. We could not eat that.

Once we killed two dogs and ate them. The men only. We gave our rice to the girls. Next day my stomach is full, I can work. After we dig garden in the fall, they let us pick up anything they don't want. So we keep alive, some of us. Some of us died, and sometimes I think I, too, would die like the others and never see my home again.

When we were there, I used to think Japan must be one of the poorest countries in whole world. In that town of Otaru of about twenty-five thousand people,[20] not one painted house did I see. One house only had a coat of tar. Everyone worked, and worked every day. Young boys and girls worked in the factories near the house where we lived.

Alex Prossoff, 1947 (1988): One day I went up to the old Jap who was kind to us and asked him which side was winning, and he said the Japs were getting weak. They had plenty men but no guns and things to fight with. I saw some big Jap cruisers, two destroyers while there, but one battleship. The officers had good clothing,

---

[20] Otaru's population in 1920 was 102,462 (Irish 2009:227) and in 1940 it was 164,282 (Demographics of Imperial Japan 2011).

but the soldiers poor, except their shoes. The officers slapped their men, sometimes hard in the face for a little thing, maybe a gun not clean or something. I notice Jap soldier does not have much freedom. On Attu most were young, twenty-five or nineteen years old. In Japan they were maybe fifty or older.

We did not have much clothing. All I had was one pair of pants, two shirts, one pair of socks, and one towel in two years.

One old Jap who talked some Russian and English was kind to us. Sometimes we would give him a piece of clothing to sell, and he would get us a little food.

We had to learn to talk Japanese, even the little children. Japs said they would kill us if we didn't. Sometimes we were beaten and our women whipped. Julia Golodoff once went three days without food to eat or water to drink. This was her punishment for talking back to the Japs and blaming them when her little girl died. She said it was Japs' fault. They made her shovel snow when she was barefoot, too. She did not die.

I had arguments with the guards over their gods. One of them wanted me to pray to their gods, but I told him I would pray to my own God. I asked them where were their gods, but they could not tell me. I saw many statues of the gods they pray to. Most were of Buddha, though. They had a funny custom of taking a dragon-like piece of wood into their houses and talking while they open and shut its big fiery mouth. What they say I don't know. Another custom was to send men with big umbrella-like hats and dressed in white to our camp. They held out small cup and begged for money. Finally guards told them it's no use; we did not have any money.

Return and Resettlement

One day the policeman who guarded the Attuans told them that the war was over. The Attuans painted the letters "POW" on the roof of their building so the American planes would know where they were. Planes flew over, dropping drums filled with delicious food. Nick Golodoff particularly remembers the canned peaches they brought. Some Japanese sources recalled that the Attuans defied orders to share some of the food and cigarettes with their friends among the Japanese guards (Stewart 1978:34).

After the Attuans heard the war was over, they were able to leave their quarters and walk around the city (Lokanin 1988:239). When they left, about two weeks later, police officer Shikanai and his superior, Sergeant Endo, accompanied the Attuans as far as Chitose air base. The Unangan requested that Mr. Shikanai come with them further, to Atgusi air base outside of Tokyo, and he did (Stewart 1978:35–36).[21]

The Attuans were given the cremated remains of those who had died in Japan, and they put all the boxes of bones of those who had died together in a big box (Lokanin 1988:239). Unfortunately, the bones were lost on the way back to the United States. Alex Prossoff said that while they were in Okinawa, the Attuans left all their baggage, including the box of bones, inside a big fence. After a big storm, the box and all the rest of their things were gone (Prossoff 1988:248). The box of remains was eventually recovered and sent to Atka. The cremated remains of the deceased Attuans were buried near the Atka church, but outside of the church grounds because the Russian Orthodox Church does not allow cremation.

The Attuans got on a plane, the first flight any of them had ever been on. They stayed in Osaka one night, then went on to Okinawa. A huge storm grounded them there for several weeks. Then they flew to Manila, where they stayed in army tents and were taken around by military men. They boarded a ship and set out for San Francisco. It took ten or eleven days, Nick Golodoff remembers, but it seemed like forever. Some government or Red Cross workers met the boat and took the Attuans to a hotel, giving them money for lodging and clothing. They were in San Francisco for a week or ten days and did a lot of walking around.

The Attuans took a train to Seattle, the first train trip any of them had taken. In that city, they attended services at the Greek Orthodox Church of the Assumption, which Alex Prossoff called the Church of Seven Domes. Some of the people went to the hospital in Tacoma (Prossoff 1988:248) for treatment of tuberculosis. The remaining Attu residents finally boarded a boat to return to the Aleutians on December 12, 1945. They got to Unalaska on the nineteenth and from there traveled to Atka with a stop in Adak (Lokanin 1988:240). They had hoped to return to Attu, but they were told there weren't enough people left to resettle their village. Sixteen Attu survivors arrived in Atka on December 21.

When the military transport ship *David W. Branch* brought them to Atka, the residents of that village were still in the process of rebuilding their village, which the US Army had burned after the residents were relocated to Southeast Alaska in 1942. The Attuans had to stay with Atkan families until the military could build houses for them. Fortunately, Nick Golodoff's mother Olean was from Atka, so she and her children Nick, Greg, and Elizabeth were able to stay with their relatives,

---

[21] Before they left Otaru, according to Henry Stewart and based on interviews with Japanese sources, Mr. Shikanai had a tailor make a suit of clothes for each of the Attuans. At Atgusi, however, the Americans gave the Attuans new clothes and made them burn the ones they were wearing (Stewart 1978:35).

the Snigaroffs. Later, Olean married an Atka man; Innokenty Golodoff married an Atka woman and began raising a family (see photos p. 81). Willie Golodoff was reunited with his wife, Julia, but then, like several others, had to go to a hospital in Tacoma (Jolis 1994:20). Four Attu "children," including eighteen-year-old John Golodoff and twenty-year-old Angelina Hodikoff, were sent to vocational school in Eklutna. One of the teachers there wrote an article about these Attu survivors. She said Angelina carried with her a scrap of paper that said:

> Father, Mike Hodkoff, burn [sic] at Attu, died in Jap camp at Otturu Island of Hokhaida. Mother, Anicia Prokoppoff, born at Attu, died at Attu, 1940. Three brothers, two named George and Leonty, Mike died when Japs came. Another brother George died in Jap camp. Sisters Mary and Annie died at Attu when the Japs came. Brother Stephen age 14, birthday Jan. 16th, taken prisoner, now thought to be at Atka. (Butts 1948)

The Attuans were unhappy that they could not return to their home. Alan May, who had visited Attu in 1936, corresponded after the war with several of the Attu people who were hospitalized with tuberculosis in Washington state. Mike Lokanin wrote to him that he missed Mike Hodikoff and his smile and that he was worried about his wife and his friend John Hodikoff, both of whom also had tuberculosis and were in another hospital. Mike Lokanin did not think the Attuans and Atkans were getting along very well with each other yet. He wrote, "We rather be on Attu instead Atka" (Lokanin 1949). Ted Bank, a visitor to Atka in 1948, said one of the troubles the Attuans had in their new home was that the Atkans wouldn't allow them to use their wood to build new houses. The Attuans thought the Atkans looked down on them (Bank 1956:78).

By June 1947, only eleven Attu survivors were at Atka. One was at Fort Richardson in the Army (John Golodoff), four were at Tacoma Hospital (Willie Golodoff, Annie Hodikoff, John Hodikoff, and Mary Prokopeuff), and six students were at Mt. Edgecombe (Sergei Artumonoff, Marina Hodikoff, Martha Hodikoff, Stephen Hodikoff, Agnes Prosoff, and Fekla Prosoff). Angelina Hodikoff had moved to Dillingham.

One consequence of the move to Atka was the exacerbation of rivalry in basketry between the villages. The Attuans and Atkans had different basket-weaving styles and kept them secret from each other. The Attuan women no longer had access to their favorite kind of grass (Shapsnikoff and Hudson 1974:50). The Attuan style, previously known as the finest form of Unangan basketry, died out with the Attuan women. Attu also once had a distinct dialect of Unangam Tunuu, but with the death of so many Attuan speakers, the dialect was no longer spoken.

Olean Prokopeuff (Golodoff), 1981: The people continued to die. All that was left was just a few of us. Time passed until we heard an airplane. We went out and we stepped out to look. We saw drums coming down in parachutes, and evidently, the plane was an American plane and the drums contained food. So we stayed up and ate all night.

Alex Prossoff, 1947 (1988): One day, 1945, we learned from hearing Japs talking that Germany has lost the war. So I went to friendly Jap and ask him if it is true Germany lose the war, and he said yes. He said the Americans now have Germany. The Japs seem very sad over Germany losing.

After that we had blackouts every night. They put us to work digging trenches. One day in August, while we were digging a trench in front of a policeman's house, we hear noise from radio coming from open window. We know enough Jap to know it is Jap emperor telling his people that Japan had lost the war. He told them they must now work very hard to live. That afternoon, the Jap guard tell us to stop working. They did not tell us war is over, but we know it because things change. Japs take their things out of caves where they had them stored. They said it is because of nice weather and they want to dry stored clothing. There are no more blackouts, either. I asked them why did they turn on lights at night and where are the sirens that used to blow when enemy planes are near. They said the Americans are over on the southern side of Japan now, so lights don't bother. But not once did they tell us they lost the war.

Seven days later a B-29 flew over very low and saw the POW sign the Japs built for us. They circled it four times and then flew so low we could see people leaning out. They dropped drums of food, candy, and cigarettes, also two bundles of clothing and shoes. The next week they came again and dropped more things. Three weeks later, three Americans came. It was then we were really happy! The Japs tried to make the Americans think they had been good to us. They had our camp cleaned up and gave the Americans good food. We told our stories before the Americans and the Japs. We told of the beatings they had given us, of the months of cold and sickness and starvation. We told of our people who died of neglect. When we finished, the Japs tore up their stories they had ready.

The Americans told us not to take any more orders from the Japs. We were free! They told us an American plane would take us away in two weeks. We did not work for Japs now. We went walking all over this city that had been our home for three years. One day four of us went walking and saw a church that looked like our own church at Attu, with big dome and a Russian cross. We walked all around the church but could not get in. We knocked at the door for a long time. Then someone come. What a surprise! Gray hair and blue eyes!

"Is this a Russian church?" I asked.

"Yes," answered the old couple in English.

"May we come in?"

"Of course. Where do you come from?" they asked. "Come in."

"We come from Attu, Alaska," I said.

"Where is that?" they ask. "Come in."

We went in and found a map. On it is little dot—Attu. We show them where we come from. They say, "Oh! You are Americans! What can we do for you boys?"

"We want to go to church," I tell them. I tell them we have been Japs' prisoners three years. Only church we have is little holy picture Mike sneak with him.

"All right," old couple say. "Come back tomorrow."

So next day we all went back and had church. It was very nice to have church again in a church like ours. The old couple told us their name was Soffieff. These old people came from Russia many years before. They lived in China before they came to Japan. They suffered very much in the war, too.

We went and had church with these old people once more before we left Otaru. Before we are going to leave Otaru, I go to Japs and say, "We want money for work we do." They finally give me handful of little paper bills, fifty-yen size. I divide among my people. When time to go, we ask for kind old Jap man. We take up collection for him, and he go home happy.

After the food was dropped, the Americans came. We could see cars running around, and they made a lot of smoke. These cars had to be cranked to get them started. So one got tired of cranking a car before it could be started. They also had some cars that didn't make any noise at all when running.

Then we were taken inside the house. We were asked if we wanted to go home. We all said, "Yes!" They were Americans, and they told us that the war was over, and we were going to be taken home. That next day, we were taken to the airport. We stayed there for three nights. Our flight must have been late or something. I never did find out.

Innokenty Golodoff, 1966: About September 1945, the Red Cross helped us leave Otaru. An American army plane took us to Okinawa. We had a big sake party at Otaru just before we left. Our policeman got drunk too. We wanted to take him with us, so they let him go to Okinawa with us then they took him back. When we left our house at Otaru we didn't use the doors, we went out through the windows because everyone was feeling so good. A Jap civilian gave us the sake, two or three bottles, almost a gallon in each one. I like sake. That was the only party we had while we were in Japan.

Olean Prokopeuff (Golodoff), 1981: We finally departed from that place and we landed on a number of islands. I don't even know the names of the islands.

We saw where the Americans dropped their atomic bomb. It looked like a bundle of kindling wood. The place appeared demolished when viewed from the airplane. When we were in Japan, we used to be evacuated to the interior whenever the Americans dropped their bombs.

Then we flew once more. I still can't remember the names of the three islands [over which we flew]. I think we were still flying, and I remembered Okinawa, because we were there for two and a half weeks. Then once again we were airborne, heading for the mainland. When we arrived on the mainland, it was unbearably hot there.

We caught a boat from Manila bound for San Francisco. During our trip, we encountered a storm, and we were told that we were in Alaska waters. We were hoping that they could let us off at Unalaska, but instead the boat continued on to San Francisco.

Alex Prossoff, 1947 (1988): At the end of two weeks, we get on C-47 and fly to Okinawa. We take all our little boxes of dead in one big box, our church books, and our trunks. The pilots flew over Nagasaki and showed us where atom bomb dropped. It is very awful! Nothing left of that big city.

At Okinawa all our boxes and things are put inside big wire fence. We had bad tornado there and when storm is over we look for our things, but big box of all our dead people, everything is gone. Someone tell us they will look for our things, and they put us on transport boat *Brewster* for San Francisco. Then I really felt I was going home.

Innokenty Golodoff, 1966: When we got back to the States, we went to San Francisco—on a navy boat. We stayed in a hotel and the Red Cross took care of us and took us to see the city and we went across the Gold[en] Gate Bridge. We stayed there for about two weeks, then we went to Seattle.

Alex Prossoff, 1947 (1988): San Francisco! That is very beautiful city, I think. It looks like heaven to me. Of all the cities I've been in, I like that one best. Red Cross and welfare people are at the boat, and doctors, and nurses. They take us to

Lankershim Fifth Street Hotel[22] and give us money to pay our hotel fare and buy food and clothing. Miss Van Every[23] of Indian Affairs took us around in her car to see things. But mostly we walk. We walk all day, Elizabeth and me, just looking. Elizabeth wear out two pair shoes and heel off one. He [sic] look very funny walking with heel off, but we walk till I see sign of little hammer hitting heel and we go there. It's a shoemaker place and he fix his heel. Then, we walk some more. Elizabeth always see things he wants. "I want this, and this and this," he say. We were in San Francisco one week and two days, and we were so busy walking and looking, we did not have time to go to church.

Innokenty Golodoff, 1966: In Seattle we stayed near White Center. We had a good time—first we stayed in a hotel, then in a camp—a house with kitchen and everything. I stayed with my brother's family.

Alex Prossoff, 1947 (1988): When we went to Seattle, we went to Church of Seven Domes. Some of our people go to hospital in Tacoma. We stay in Seattle many days, then we get on boat *Branch* and come to Atka. We want to go to Attu. They tell us soldiers still on Attu and no more village. We must come to Atka. They will give us new house here.

Olean Prokopeuff (Golodoff), 1981: From San Francisco we took a train to Seattle. From Seattle we boarded a ship, *Branch*, and later arrived at Adak. When we were in Seattle, we were there for some time, and it was getting close to Christmas. We did not really want to go home, but we were brought here. At that time, they dropped off many soldiers on Adak. We were brought here from Adak in a small tug. I had gotten used to the big ship that brought us from Seattle, and I did not feel very safe on that small tug.

When the tug arrived at Atka, a truck picked us up and we were taken to the school. At the school, we were assigned to where we were going to live. I was placed in Cedor's house. A year passed, then the houses were built for us. Army Quonset huts were made for us to live in, and we stayed in the huts for another year. Then our houses were finished so we moved in. Since then, they have been our houses for a long time. Today, whenever there is a storm, I don't trust my poor house.

Innokenty Golodoff, 1966: After Seattle we went to Adak and stayed there one night, then they took us to Atka. The new houses were already built. The

---

[22] The Hotel Lankershim was a large and well-known hotel on Fifth Street in San Francisco OK(Brusca 2010).

[23] Mildred van Every worked as a matron for the BIA's San Francisco office between 1934 and 1946.

Attu children taking communion in Seattle. *Becky Bendixon, via Ebay*

government built them for us. We tried to go to Attu, but they told us we were not enough people, so the government wouldn't let us go to Attu. The government told us to live with the Atka people. So we got to Atka on December 11, 1945. Then I was single, but today I have a wife and three kids, two girls and a boy. My oldest girl is nineteen, and my youngest, the boy, is sixteen. Now the Attu people like it at Atka. My wife is an Atka woman, and I don't want to go back to Attu.

Nick's Connection to Japan

A Japanese author named Masami Sugiyama has written a book about Nick and the other Attuans, published in Japan in 1987. The English translation of the title on the cover is "Meetings between Aleutian and Japanese People," although the book has also been called in English "On the Trail of the Picture." The author was inspired by a picture he saw of Nick Golodoff, then six years old, riding on the back of a Japanese soldier. The picture was taken in 1942 by Kiri Sugiyama (no relationship to Masami Sugiyama), a military photographer who accompanied the Japanese soldiers on Attu. In the early 1980s, to research his book, Masami Sugiyama traveled to Atka to meet surviving Attuans who still lived there. He also went to Otaru, on Hokkaido Island, to visit the places the Attuans had stayed

Nick's mother Olean with her new husband, Ralph Prokopeuff, on their wedding day in 1947. *Nick Golodoff*

Innokenty and Vasha Golodoff, with their baby, "Toughie" [Helen], on their wedding day in 1947. *UW Press, Ethel Ross Oliver*

and to look for the Japanese people who had known them in those days. When he met Masami in Atka, Nick Golodoff called him "Sam" because it was easier to pronounce than his full name. When Nick went back to Japan in 1995, he met Sam in Tokyo.

Nick was invited to go to Japan in 1995 to attend a conference on wartime compensation. All his travel expenses were paid so that he could speak at the conference on behalf of the Attuans. A number of newspapers and TV stations ran stories about Nick, and he still has some of the clippings about his visit to Japan. After his trip, he received calls and letters from all over the world. While he was in Japan, Nick visited the places he and the other Attuans had stayed in Otaru. He met with a doctor who had treated the Attuans, who although quite elderly was still working. Nick asked for the medical records from his father's stay in the infirmary and subsequent death, but was told that giving them to him would be against the law.

Sylvia Kobayashi from Anchorage came with Nick to Japan and acted as his translator. Both she and her husband had been in Japanese-American internment camps in the United States during World War II. In Japan, some people asked Nick if Mrs. Kobayashi was his wife!

While in Japan, Nick also visited the soldier who had carried Nick on his back in Attu when Nick was a little boy. He met the soldier, Mr. Kamani, and his wife in Tokyo. Since 1995, the soldier has passed away.

Hiroko Harada, a professor of Japanese at the University of Alaska Anchorage, has written a summary in English of parts of Masami Sugiyama's book. It contains

Deceased before November 27, 1945		
Name	Born	Died
Artumonoff, John	1882	1942 on Attu
Artumonoff, Mavra	1924	1944
Artumonoff, Peter	1920	1944
Borenin, Annie Golodoff	1919	1943
Golodoff, Artelion "Arty" (Angelina's baby)	1943 in Japan	1943 in Japan
Golodoff, Harman (Garman)	1888	1945
Golodoff, Helen	1929	1944
Golodoff, Lavrenti	1900	1945
Golodoff, Leonty	1931	1943
Golodoff, Mary	1895	1943
Golodoff, Michael (Julia's baby)	1943 in Japan	1943 in Japan
Golodoff, Valvigian (Valirjian)	1939	1943
Hodikoff, Anecia (Mike H.'s baby)	1943 in Japan	1943 in Japan
Hodikoff, Fred (Fedosay)	1901	1945
Hodikoff, George	1929	1945
Hodikoff, Michael Gorga "Mike" (chief)	1893	1945
Lokanin, Gabriel (Mike L.'s baby)	1944 in Japan	1944 in Japan
Lokanin, Tatiana	1941	1944
Prokopioff, Anecia Kriukov (Golodoff)	1886	1942 while underway for Japan
Prokopioff, Mary	1929	1943
Prossoff, Bladimir	1932	1943
Prossoff, Martha Hodikoff	1903	1943

FIG. 6. Attu residents who died in Japan and those who survived. *Murray 2005; Oliver 1988*

Surviving as of November 27, 1945		
Name	Born	Died
Artumonoff, Sergi, 19	1927	last record in 1966
Golodoff (Prokopioff), Alfred Jr., infant	1945 in Japan	
Golodoff (Prossoff), Thecla (Fekla), 10	1935	
Golodoff, Elizabeth, 3	1941	
Golodoff, Gregory, 6	1940	
Golodoff, Innokinty "Popeye", 28	1917	1998
Golodoff, John, 18	1927	2009
Golodoff, Julia Prokopeuff, 24	1923	1954
Golodoff, Mary Tarkanoff Lokanin, 28	1918	before 1963
Golodoff, Nick, 9	1935	2013
Golodoff, Olean, 5	1939	
Golodoff, Olean Horosoff, 36	1911	
Golodoff, Willie, 37	1918	1983
Hodikoff, Angelina, 19	1927	1981
Hodikoff, Annie Yatchmenoff, 28	1918	disappears from records in Tacoma hospital 1945
Hodikoff, John, 21	1927	
Hodikoff, Marina, 7	1938	1996
Hodikoff, Martha, 9	1937	
Hodikoff, Stephen, 14	1931	1985
Lokanin, Mike, 33	1912	1961
Lokanin, Parascovia Horosoff, 23	1922	1994
Prokopioff (Golodoff), Alfred Sr., 38	1908	1963 (or 1974?)
Prossoff, Agnes, 6	1940	1980
Prossoff, Alexy, 29	1916	before 1949
Prossoff, Elizabeth Prokopioff Golodoff, 27	1919	

valuable information about the Attuans' stay in Japan from the perspective of the Japanese policemen, doctors, and nurses who had contact with them. Sugiyama also visited both places where the Attuans had stayed in Otaru, the railroad dormitory in Wakatake-cho and the Shinto priests' quarters in Shimizu-cho. During his 1995 trip to Japan, Nick was able to visit the house in Wakatake-cho, but the house in Shimizu-cho and the clay mine where the Attuans had worked were both gone.

Here are some of the people Masami Sugiyama interviewed in Japan:

- Takeshiro Shikanai—police officer who lived with the Attuans and was their friend. He spoke the Tsugaru dialect and taught Japanese to Elizabeth Prossoff. When the Attuans were released, Shikanai accompanied them as far as Atsuki. Shikanai's wife was Toki Shikanai, who died in 1978. Takeshiro Shikanai had already died when Nick visited in 1995.

- Toshikatsu Endo—higher ranking police officer who arrived at the Otaru Police Station later in the war. He may be the officer "E," mentioned by Henry Stewart, who was harsher in his dealings with the Attuans and hit Angelina Hodikoff in the leg with a rock because she would not do housework or laundry at the house.

- Ms. Moto—a nurse who remembered Attuans hospitalized at the Otaru Tuberculosis Clinic, especially a woman named "Arsa" and a two-year-old named Elizabeth.

- Ms. Kusakabe—a nurse at the tuberculosis clinic. Innokenty Golodoff remembered her as "Kasha-san" and called her his girlfriend.

- Ken Hattori—a linguist teaching at Hokkaido Imperial University, who visited the Attuans in summer 1943 and researched their language.

- Dr. Mikio Ishibashi—director of the Ishibashi Hospital, who treated one Attuan who was infected with diphtheria.

- Dr. Minoru Yamauchi—treated the Attuans at the Otaru Tuberculosis Clinic. He remembered Mike Lokanin very well and was friends with him.

- Dr. Noguchi—the director of the Otaru Tuberculosis Clinic.

- Yuriko Tanaka—head nurse at the Otaru Tuberculosis Clinic.

EPILOGUE

In October 2012, the few surviving Attu residents, and thirty descendants from widely scattered places in Alaska and outside, gathered in Anchorage for an Attu reunion, part of the National Park Service's Lost Villages of the Aleutians project. Nick Golodoff and his brother Greg Golodoff participated in the event; their sister Elizabeth was unable to take part but was represented by her husband, George Kudrin. These siblings, the only remaining Attuans who had experienced captivity in Japan, were treated with great respect and pride at the reunion. The National Park Service had published Nick's memoir a few months earlier, and there was much interest in his story. Nick signed copies of *Attu Boy*, was honored with an award for his book from the Alaska Historical Society, and was interviewed by TV and newspaper reporters. His granddaughter Brenda Maly, who had helped him compile his memories over several years, also attended the reunion.

The Aleutian-Pribilof Island Association hosted a dinner, reception, and culture camp for the Attuans on the second day of the reunion, with the express purpose of welcoming them to the Unangan community. Several in the group were moved to tears when a Russian Orthodox choir performed "Memory Eternal," a song associated with funerals, to commemorate the village of Attu and its former residents. At the last night's reception, an Unangan dance group, the Atka Dancers, performed. They invited the Attu reunion attendees to dance with them, and some did, including one who danced from his wheelchair.

At the reunion, the descendants of Attu made new connections with living relatives and honored those who perished. By renewing memories of the prewar village where the Attuans had been happy and healthy, and by helping them understand the Attuans' traumatic ordeal in Japan, the Attu reunion, centered around Nick and *Attu Boy*, brought the participants closer to a shared identity as Unangan descendants of Attu.

The participants at the reunion were especially grateful to Nick for telling his story and allowing them to gain knowledge of their parents' and grandparents' experiences. After the war, several of the Attuans who survived captivity had left Alaska and married non-Natives. They did not talk about the experience in Japan, and their children never learned about it from them. The publication of *Attu Boy* allowed the descendants of Attu to see pictures of the old village and its residents, including their own relatives, sometimes for the first time.

Nick died three months after the Attu reunion, on February 8, 2013, and was laid to rest in Atka.

APPENDIX:
ATTU PREHISTORY AND HISTORY

Attu's remote beauty has always impressed visitors, but its beauty is often hidden by fog, wind, and rain. In a 1994 student paper, Jennifer Jolis wrote:

> Attu Island. Forty-two miles long, fifteen miles wide, mist-enshrouded, wind-whipped, mountainous, and mysterious, it lies at the western end of the Aleutian chain of islands, which curve across the top of the North Pacific like jewels in a necklace, connecting North America with its past. These volcanic islands are the crest of a submarine ridge approximately 1,400 miles long, twenty to sixty miles wide, and twelve thousand feet high above the ocean floor to either side. The islands separate the North Pacific Ocean to the south from the Bering Sea to the north. Coming together over the islands these systems clash and mingle, giving rise to climatic conditions that have earned them the sobriquet "birthplace of the winds." At any time of year warm, moist air from the Pacific, meeting the frigid arctic air of the Bering Sea, can produce gale force winds, dense fog to sea level, or brilliantly clear sunny skies, followed in moments by rain squalls and more fog. Attu is the westernmost island in this arc; indeed, the westernmost point in North America. At longitude 173 degrees East, it lies over 1,100 miles from the mainland of Alaska and less than 550 miles from the Kamchatka Peninsula of Russia. The island's volcanic origins have produced a terrain of steep mountains rising from a deeply indented coastline with an abundance of bays and inlets. In summer, wildflowers bloom in brilliant profusion in the alpine tundra, a lovely surprise for anyone who looks closely: orchid, monkshood, lupine, rhododendron. The British botanist Isobel Hutchison collected sixty-nine species in less than two hours at the end of the 1936 season and estimated that a complete sampling would rival Unalaska's 350 species. The long beach grasses bend and sway to the earth before the winds that sweep across the

hills, mimicking the waves in the coves and bays. On foggy evenings the calls of loons and eiders sound lonely, lost, otherworldly. The upwelling produced by the convergence of the northern and southern waters around the islands produces a marine life of great richness and variety. The sea is home to sea otters, sea lions, harbor seals, the occasional whale, migrating waterfowl and gulls, halibut, salmon, greenling, flounder. Although numbers of all species have diminished over time, the area continues to be one of the most rich and productive in the world, boasting the world's largest number of sea mammal species. (Jolis 1994:3)

Attu Prehistory[24]

Attu is one of the Near Islands, so named because they are the nearest Aleutian Islands to Russia and Asia. They are not very near to the mainland of Alaska; Atka, the closest village in that direction, is five hundred miles away. In spite of being so far from mainland Alaska, a surprising amount of archaeological work has been attempted in the Near Islands. Most of the work has emphasized the distinctive culture of the Near Island Unangan.

Beginning in 1874 William H. Dall (1877), a surveyor with the Coast Survey, excavated village sites on Attu, Agattu, and Amchitka as well as islands further east. He was followed by Waldemar Jochelson (1925), leading an expedition sponsored by the Imperial Russian Geographical Society and the wealthy Riaboushinsky family. His team spent nineteen months in the Aleutian Islands, excavating sites on Unalaska, Umnak, Atka, and Attu. In 1909, they excavated three sites on Attu. One, a post-Russian site they called "Sin," was near the twentieth-century winter village on Chichagof Bay. A second site, also from the historical era, was near the summer village at Sarana Bay. At the third, called Nanikax, on Lastova Bay, the crew found fifteen pits (Jochelson 1925:24). A typical prehistoric Unangan winter settlement consisted of a few large houses with several families in each. Summer homes, less permanent, were smaller and housed only one family (Corbett 1990:9). Jochelson found human remains in kitchen midden near the village sites, but later research indicated that most burials were in specially constructed houses within the village. Unlike other Unangan, it appeared the people living in the Near Islands did not use caves for burials or practice mummification (Jochelson 1925:46; Laughlin and Marsh 1951:82).

---

[24] Adapted from *People at the End of the World* by Debra Corbett et al., 2010

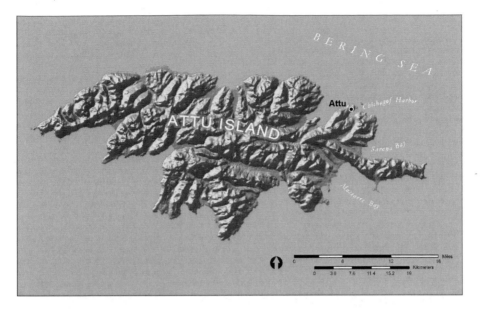

FIG. 7. Map of Attu Island. *Adapted from National Park Service 2011. Base image from SRTM Shaded Relief (Eastern North) ESRI.*

Aleš Hrdlička (1945), a physical anthropologist at the Smithsonian Institution, spent a summer working on Agattu. A member of Hrdlička's field team, Alan May, excavated a site near the village in Chichagof Harbor.

In the 1950s, after the war, Albert Spaulding (1962) excavated at Krugloi Point, Agattu. Since then, most professional work in the Near Islands has consisted of site surveys, notably by Ted Bank II in 1948 and the National Park Service in 1968 (McCartney 1974). In 1975, to aid in their Alaska Native Claims Settlement Act applications for historic and cemetery sites, the Aleut Corporation contracted with Bruno Frohlich and David Kopjansky to survey the coast of Attu, where they found twelve archaeological sites. In 1985, the US Bureau of Indian Affairs (BIA) began investigating these claims in the western Aleutians on Amchitka in the Rat Islands. The Civil Rights Act of 1988 led to the BIA investigation of the historic village on Attu. BIA surveyed the rest of the Near Islands in 1988 and 1989. Corbett (1990) tested several sites on Shemya Island. In 1997, the Western Aleutians Archaeological and Paleobiological Project began fourteen years of work to understand the history and lives of the Near Island Unangan. The teams excavated on Attu, Shemya, Buldir, Rat, and Little Kiska Islands. The report for the work on Shemya has been published (Corbett et al. 2010); the rest of the work is still being analyzed.

Most archaeologists agree that the Aleutians were settled from the east. The origins of the Near Island Unangan may be found in many places, but their deep roots as maritime hunters are found on the Alaska Peninsula and eastern Aleutians. More than nine thousand years ago, land-based hunters developed the skills and technology to hunt sea mammals and fish offshore.

The earliest evidence of human occupation of the Aleutians, dated to about eight thousand years ago, is on Anangula Island in the eastern Aleutians (Laughlin and Marsh 1951). Recently, Anangula-style sites have been found in Unalaska Bay (Knecht and Davis 2001). The distinctive tool kit consists of long, narrow, parallel-sided blades; burins for carving bone; and end and side scrapers. This technology is a variant of the widespread Paleo-Arctic tradition found throughout Alaska and parts of Siberia.

About seven thousand years ago, sites at Umnak and Akun still showed a relationship with Anangula but people had added stemmed points, bifacial tools, and shallow semisubterranean houses. Dumond (2001) suggests this tradition shares similarities with the Ocean Bay tradition of Kodiak and the Alaska Peninsula.

By five thousand years ago, there were people in the Rat Islands, but as far as we know the Near Islands were still uninhabited. Between three and four thousand years ago, a distinct Margaret Bay tradition appears on Unalaska and neighboring islands. The most notable aspect of this tradition is houses with stone walls, clay floors, and sophisticated fireplaces with external vents, chimneys, and subfloor channels (Knecht and Davis 2001). By three thousand years ago, the Aleutian tradition as it is widely recognized was fully developed.

While the area could have been occupied as early as 2000 BC (Bureau of Indian Affairs 1988:8–9), we will never know exactly when the first exploring parties landed on the Near Islands. They came from the east, from the Rat Islands. Young men, proving themselves, explored the new islands. These pristine islands with untapped hunting grounds must have electrified the people. By three thousand years ago, there were several settlements in the Near Islands. The earliest colonists settled in areas with the richest resources: at Massacre Bay on Attu, at Aga Cove and Krugloi Point on Agattu, on the south coast of Shemya, and where Alaid and Nizki connect.

Early inhabitants hunted fur seals in local rookeries and caught huge cod at sea. A thousand years later, smaller reef fish and shellfish were more common. This switch prompted an increase in the use of small, jewel-like bone fishhooks to catch the smaller prey. The tool kit also changed. The oldest sites contain more large cobble tools, including hammerstones, choppers, and abraders. Later, there is an increase in cutting and scraping tools. A variety of drills and chisels, ground stone knives, and adzes appear. Bone tools became more elaborate, with new styles of harpoon and spear points and awls and the addition of fishing gorges and woodworking chisels to the toolkit. The appearance of jewelry and other decorative pieces signals increased status differences between individuals.

Populations in the early settlements were small, but by 2,400 years ago had grown dramatically and many new villages appeared. The early villages were made up of a few houses, each occupied by an extended family, maybe thirty to forty people. Before about a thousand years ago, there were probably about two thousand people in the Near Islands. Major cultural changes occurred sometime about 750 years ago. The population grew to possibly four times the size it had been earlier. Villages lined the coastlines of all the islands, some with several hundred inhabitants. In each village, one or two houses were substantially larger than the others. Larger communities need more formal leadership than family-based hamlets. When the Russians arrived in 1745, they reported that village chiefs built large houses to care for orphans and the poor and for communal ceremonies.

The Near Island culture was firmly rooted in the ancestral Aleutian tradition, extending back to Anangula and even further to the Alaska Peninsula. At the western end of the Aleutian Islands they were free to develop their own unique traditions, and their culture became one of the most distinctive variants of the historic Unangan people. The Sasignan were the Unangan group that inhabited the Near Islands, including the people of Attu, Agattu, and the Semichi Islands (Bergsland and Dirks 1990:2).

Russian Colonialization

Because the Near Islands were the closest populated lands to Russia, the people of those islands were the first to be contacted in the eighteenth century. Crews of *promyshlenniki* (fur hunters and traders) that included both Russians and Kamchadals were assembled in the Russian Far East to travel to the Aleutians (Laughlin 1984:315).

With the arrival of Russian fur hunters off Agattu in September 1745, the world of the Aleuts changed forever. The Russian crew was met on shore by a hundred armed men and moved instead to the less populated Attu Island (Berkh 1974:16). The Russians captured an old woman and a boy, keeping the boy to train as translator. Within a few weeks, a Russian party attacked another settlement and killed fifteen men to get women. These violent acts are recorded by the names Murder Point and Massacre Bay on Attu.

Between 1745 and 1799, eighty Russian hunting parties worked in the Near Islands, mostly on Attu. In 1750, Andreian Tolstykh introduced arctic fox to Attu Island from the Commander Islands. In many places in the Aleutian Islands, the company encouraged the introduction of breeding pairs of foxes as crop animals (Black 1984:101–102).

Because the initial Russian hunting pressure was concentrated in the western Aleutians, the sea mammal population declined quickly in the Near Islands. The hunters went further east, to the Fox Islands, where there were more sea otters and foxes. They continued to stop in the Near Islands to collect tribute and to press the residents into service as hunters (BIA 1988:17).

The effects of contact were devastating. Within a few years, the population had declined greatly because of disease and because of the hardship of forced labor for the Russians (BIA 1988:18). By 1762, the merchants Cherepanov and Kul'kov estimated a total population of one hundred for the island group (Liapunova 1979).

Each island had its own chief. Agattu was politically dominant at contact, but by the 1760s, power had shifted to Attu. Chief Bakutan and his second chief Chintuyach were based on Attu, and most people had moved to that island. The move was prompted by many factors, including population collapse, a desire to be near the Russians and their trade goods, and protection by the Russian presence from raids by their eastern neighbors (Black 1984:73).

In 1799, the Russian government granted the Russian-American Company a twenty-year monopoly on the Pacific fur trade. The Attuans remained independent of company control; they hunted for themselves and traded with the Russians. By the end of the eighteenth century, the small community, with twenty able-bodied men, occupied two settlements: one in Massacre Bay and the other at the mouth of Chichagof Harbor.

In 1805, the Russians moved people from Adak or Amchitka, called Atkans,[25] to Attu. They built a company settlement at the head of Chichagof Harbor. A visitor in 1811 reported poor conditions in the new settlement. No ship had stopped there for five years, and supplies were low. Some of the Atkans had left Attu, and the only Russians remaining were the manager and one other man. The Attuans were living separately from the Atkans and were more independent of the Russian company, although they traded furs in return for goods such as thread, guns, and ammunition (Black 1984:159–161). In subsequent years, the number of Attuans decreased, while the Atkan settlement grew (BIA 1988:18-19). By 1830, the Chichagof Harbor village was the only permanent winter settlement.[26]

---

[25] Lydia Black held that the "Atkans" were really not from Atka (Debbie Corbett, pers. comm., 2011).

[26] The Russians also moved Unangan to settle the Commander Islands to the west. Between 1814 and 1816, some of the relocated "Atkans" and several Attuans were taken from Attu to the Commander Islands (Lantis in Oliver 1988:xxiv). Other transfers from Attu followed. Even after Russia's 1867 sale of Alaska, in 1872–1873 a group of thirty-eight Unangan hunters and their families, mainly from Attu, moved to the Commander Islands (Black

Although the first baptism took place on Attu in 1758, predating the arrival of Russian Orthodox clergy, it was 1825 before a chapel was in existence there. When the priest Iakov Netsvetov, a Creole of mixed Russian and Unangan descent, was appointed to head the Atka parish in 1828, his duties included regular visits to Attu and other outposts such as Amlia and Bering Island. Netsvetov made his first trip to Attu in 1831, noting at that time that the language spoken on Attu was different from the one on Atka. Netsvetov counted 120 Unangan and Creoles in a company settlement at Chichagof Harbor. All of them were baptized, but he said the Attuans were more independent and superstitious than other Unangan. At the time, most Native residents lived in barabaras (sod houses), but the village also included three houses, a store, and a chapel (Netsvetov 1980:33–34). According to his records, the priest's next visits were in 1833 and 1838 (Netsvetov 1980:79, 173–174). Local people maintained the chapel during the several years that might elapse between visits from a priest.

Sea otters were the focus of the Russian company's interest. Company hunters left for the Semichi Island hunting grounds for sea otter hunting in November and December. The hunters returned to Attu in December to trap foxes until spring. Attuans accompanied the Atkans to the Semichis and Agattu to hunt, but did not trap foxes (Khlebnikoff 1994).

After May, subsistence pursuits took over from commercial hunting. Red salmon were caught from weirs at fish camps in Sarana and Massacre Bays and dried for winter. Barrels of salmon were also salted. Men traveled along the north coast of Attu hunting driftwood, accompanied by women who fished on the reefs and gathered grass and edible plants. Sea lions and seals were hunted where and whenever found. Except for tea, sugar, molasses, and biscuits, the islanders were self-sufficient in food. They traded fox and sea otter furs for rifles, shot and powder, and fiber to make nets. The most sought-after goods were wool worsted, linen, Chinese cotton and silk, velveteen, velvet, and taffeta. Finished clothing, such as vests, shirts, trousers, caps and hats, and silk shawls, was also popular. Other necessities included cooking vessels, copper teakettles, casks, wooden beams, and needles and thread.

A Russian-American Company census of Attu in 1860 found 227 Unangan and 21 Creoles, including the company manager. About fifty men and ten women were sent out each year to hunt, and furs were shipped out at the end of each year's hunt. The village included a chapel, a wooden house, a bathhouse, a barracks, a wharf, and a store (BIA 1988:19).

1984:105). The Attuan dialect once spoken on Copper Island, one of the Commanders, was creolized, with Russian verbal inflection (Bergsland and Dirks 1990:5, 7fn).

Attu in the American Era, 1867–1942

After the sale of Alaska to the United States in 1867, a decline in services on remote islands contributed to a dramatic drop in the population. By 1880, the village had 107 inhabitants, down from 220 in 1870 (Scammon 1874; US Census 1884). The economy depended on sea otter and fox furs.

In the first decades of the twentieth century, Attu received few visits from out-siders. Those who did visit the remote island were impressed with how clean and neat the village was and how friendly and happy its residents. In 1909, Attu was one of the sites Waldemar Jochelson studied with the Aleut-Kamchatka Archeological Expedition. The party arrived June 15 and stayed in the island's winter village in Chichagof Harbor. A few days later they moved with the Unangan to Sarana Bay, the summer village, where they remained until early August (Jochelson 1925:16–17). The village teachers' files show that in the same year, 1909, there was an attempt to place reindeer on Attu as part of educator Sheldon Jackson's program to institute new ways of life among Alaska Natives. The effort to make Attuans into reindeer herders was not successful.

The 1920s brought high fox prices and prosperity to the islands. A. B. Sommerville had leased the Semichi Islands in 1911 and planted fifteen blue foxes there (Gray 1939:134). In 1922, Fred Schroeder of the Aleutian Fur Company bought Sommerville out and planted foxes on Agattu and built cabins on Shemya and Alaid (Golodoff 1988).

The Aleuts on Attu replaced their sod barabaras with frame houses (Gray 1939). A wooden church, built of materials purchased with proceeds from baskets made by seven women, was completed in the 1920s (Shapsnikoff and Hudson 1974). A school was built in 1932 (Golodoff 1988; West 1938), but no teachers arrived until 1940. Trappers left home around October to restock and repair the nine cabins around the coast of Attu. Trapping began in November and ended in March. They returned to the village in January for the holidays. The Attuans also trapped on Agattu, the Semichis, and in the Rat Islands on Rat Island proper. Islands were worked on a rotation, allowing fox populations to recover for several years before returning. Men trapping these other islands were often accompanied by their families.

Innokenty Golodoff (1988) described trapping on Shemya in 1938. Innokenty, his brother Willie, Willie's wife Julia, their children Mary and Michael, and three other adults travelled to Shemya in late fall. They took two dories, five-horsepower motors, gas lanterns, fuel, tobacco, and staples such as flour, sugar, tea, and coffee. The cabin, a one-room frame structure, was located on the eastern shore of Alcan Harbor. Each man set about ten traps and checked them on foot. They wore homemade sea lion gut raincoats and sea lion flipper boots in foul weather. When conditions permitted, they motored to Alaid and Nizki and trapped there.

The men hunted sea lions, seals, geese, and ducks on the offshore rocks around Shemya. The trappers also spent a great deal of time searching for driftwood to heat the cabin and for cooking. Trappers on the outarnoer islands could remain in camp until May before a vessel arrived to take them home (Golodoff 1988).

In the 1930s and the beginning of the 1940s, Attu was the remote and peaceful place that visitors praised and that Nick remembers from his earliest years. The trader, Fred Schroeder, was the main source of store goods, cash, and credit in return for fox furs and baskets. Contacts with the outside world came when coast guard cutters stopped every few months. In the years just before the war, when fears of the Japanese were mounting, a radio was brought to Attu, and Chief Mike Hodikoff was taught how to use it—a job Foster Jones, the teacher's husband, took over in 1941.

The Japanese invasion of the village in June 1942, and the other events related in previous chapters, ended forever the village's reputation as a remote paradise.

Conclusions

After the Attuans were taken to Japan, their village was occupied by Japanese troops and was destroyed by American bombing (Garfield 1995:213–214). On other parts of the island, the US military left behind the remains of structures, including tunnels used for storage. In 1987, a "peace memorial" was installed to honor all the soldiers who died at Attu, and in 1993 a sign was placed to commemorate the Attu villagers' wartime ordeal.

The island of Attu has remained uninhabited. There is nothing left of the wooden houses, the school, church, or the barabaras that were still in use in 1942. A Coast Guard Loran (long-range navigation system) station operated there in 1961 and was staffed by twenty personnel. It was closed in 2010 after the global positioning system (GPS) replaced Loran as a navigational system for ships and aircraft.

As Jennifer Jolis wrote two decades ago,

> Periodically, the island is visited by fishermen or by interested naturalists, biologists, and archeologists, usually in the employ of the US Fish and Wildlife Service. The buildings and bridges built by the Navy are disappearing, each year the wind and waves take back the land. Each spring the grasses continue to wave, the eiders to sound their lonely calls. A lone eagle flies over Temnac Valley. The people are gone. The island remains. (Jolis 1994:30)

BIBLIOGRAPHY

Bank II, Ted
1956   *Birthplace of the Winds.* New York: Thomas Y. Crowell Co.

Bergsland, Knut
1980   *Atkan Aleut-English Dictionary.* Anchorage: University of Alaska and National Bilingual Materials Development Center.
1994   *Aleut Dictionary: Unangam Tunudgusii.* Fairbanks: Alaska Native Language Center, University of Alaska.

Bergsland, Knut, and Moses L. Dirks (eds).
1990   *Unangam Ungiikangin Kayux Tunusangn: Aleut Tales and Narratives, Collected 1909–1910 by Waldemar Jochelson.* Fairbanks: Alaska Native Language Center, University of Alaska.

Berkh, Vasilii N.
1974   *A Chronological History of the Discovery of the Aleutian Islands or the Exploits of Russian Merchants with a Supplement of Historical Data on the Fur Trade.* Kingston, Ontario: Limestone Press.

Black, Lydia
1984   *Atka: An Ethnohistory of the Western Aleutians.* Kingston, Ontario: Limestone Press.

Breu, Mary
2009   *Last Letters from Attu: The True Story of Etta Jones, Alaska Pioneer and Japanese P.O.W.* Anchorage, AK: Alaska Northwest Books.

Brusca, Frank X.
2010   Route 40.net. Website: http://www.route40.net/page. asp?n=918, accessed 6/8/11.

Bureau of Indian Affairs (BIA), ANCSA 14(h)1 office
1988   Report of Investigation for Attu Village. Written for the Aleut Corporation, Anchorage Alaska. (There is no date on the report, but the investigations were completed in 1988.)

Butts, Rose Curtice
1948   Prisoners from Alaska. *Alaska Sportsman*, May 1948:14–15, 36–39.

Carter, Erik T.
1994   Removal and Dispossession: Aleut Prisoners of War from Attu Islands, Alaska, Interned in Japan During World War II, 1942 to 1945. Unpublished M.A. thesis, Pacific Rim Master of Arts Program, Alaska Pacific University, Anchorage, Alaska.

Corbett, Debra G.
1990   Aleut Settlement Patterns in the Western Aleutian Islands, Alaska. Unpublished M.A. thesis, Department of Anthropology, University of Alaska Fairbanks.

Corbett, Debra, Dixie West, and Christine Lefevre
2010   *People at the End of the World: The Western Aleutians Project and the Archaeology of Shemya Island.* Anchorage, AK: Alaska Anthropological Association, Aurora Monograph Series, No. 8.

Dall, William H.
1877   On Succession in the Shell-heaps of the Aleutians Islands. In *Tribes of the Extreme Northwest*, Vol. I. Contributions to North American Ethnology. Washington, DC: Government Printing Office. Pp. 41–91.

Demographics of Imperial Japan
2011   Accessed via Wikipedia, http://en.wikipedia.org/wiki.Demographics_of_Imperial_Japan

Dumond, Don E., ed.
2001   *Recent Archaeology in the Aleut Zone of Alaska.* University of Oregon Anthropological Papers 58.

Foreign Resident Population
2011   Foreign Resident Population of Japan: Nationality and District of Residents, as of June 30, 1942. Website: http:/ home.comcast.net/~winjerd/CIC/ForeignResidents, accessed 5/31/11.

Garfield, Brian
1995   *The Thousand-Mile War: World War II in Alaska and the Aleutians.* Fairbanks: University of Alaska Press.

Golodoff, Innokenty
1966   The Last Days of Attu Village. *Alaska Sportsman,* December, pp. 8–9.
1988   Interview notes, Debra Corbett and Terence Fifield, August 1988.

Gray, H. D.
1939   Proposed plans for the administration of the Aleutian Islands Wildlife Refuge. Unpublished report.

Hrdlička, Aleš
1945   *The Aleutian and Commander Islands.* Philadelphia, PA: Wistar Institute of Anatomy and Biology.

Hutchinson, Isobel Wylie
1937   *Stepping Stones from Alaska to Asia.* London: Blackie.

Irish, Ann B.
2009   *Hokkaido: A History of Ethnic Transition and Development on Japan's Northern Island.* Jefferson, NC: McFarland.

Jochelson, Waldemar
1925   *Archaeological Investigations in the Aleutian Islands.* Publication No. 367. Washington, DC: Carnegie Institution of Washington.

Jolis, Jennifer
1994   *Otherwise There is Nobody: The People of Attu Island, Alaska.* Paper submitted for class, Perspectives on the North, Department of Northern Studies, University of Alaska Fairbanks.

Jones, Etta
1946   I Am the Woman the Japs Captured in the Aleutians. Pacific Motor Boat. September 1946. Pp. 38–43, 88, 91.

Khlebnikoff, Kyrill T.
1994   Notes on Russian America. M. Ramsay, translator. Fairbanks, AK: Limestone Press.

Knecht, Richard A., and Richard S. Davis
2001   A Prehistoric Sequence for the Eastern Aleutians. In: *Recent Archaeology in the Aleut Zone of Alaska,* Don Dumond, ed. University of Oregon Anthropological Papers 58:269288.

Kohlhoff, Dean
1995   When the Wind Was a River: Aleut Evacuation in World War II. Seattle: University of Washington Press.

Laughlin, William S.
1984   Massacre at Chaluka. *Polar Record* 22(138):314318.

Laughlin, William S., and Gordon Marsh
1951   A New View of the History of the Aleutians. Arctic 4(2):75–88.

Liapunova, Rosa G.
1996   Essays on the Ethnography of the Aleuts (At the End of the Eighteenth and the First Half of the Nineteenth Century). Rasmuson Library Historical Translation Series, Vol. 9. Fairbanks, AK: University of Alaska Press.

Lokanin, Mike
1949   Letter to Alan G. May, May 23rd, 1949. In University of Alaska Anchorage, Archives & Special Collections, Papers of Alan G. May, HMC-0690.
1988   This is My Life's Story. In *Journal of an Aleutian Year*. Ethel Ross Oliver. Seattle: University of Washington Press. Pp. 220–240.

May, Alan G.
1936   Personal Journals of Smithsonian Expedition to the Aleutian Islands, 1935–1937. University of Alaska Anchorage, Archives & Special Collections, Papers of Alan G. May, HMC-0690.
1942   Attu: A Personal Account of Alaska's Community in the Far East. *Natural History*, October: 132136.

McCartney, Allen P.
1974   1972 Archaeological Site Survey in the Aleutian Islands, Alaska. In *International Conference on the Prehistory and Paleoecology of Western North American Arctic and Subarctic*. S. Raymond and P. Schledermann, eds. Calgary, Alberta: University of Calgary. Pp. 113–126.

Murray, Martha
2005   Attu. Lost Villages: Mini-biographies of the last inhabitants of Attu, Biorka, Chernofski, Kashega, and Makushin. Draft, 2 August 2005.

Naval History Online
2011   NavSource Naval History Archives. Accessed June 4, 2011.

Netsvetov, Iakov
1980   The Journals of Iakov Netsvetov: The Atkha Years, 1828–1844. Translated, with an introduction and supplementary material, by Lydia Black. Kingston, Ontario: Limestone Press.

Nutchuk [Simeon Oliver] with Alden Hatch
1946   *Back to the Smoky Sea*. New York: Julian Messner.

Oliver, Ethel Ross
1988   Journal of an Aleutian Year. Seattle: University of Washington Press. Appendix 1: Mike Lokanin's story, pp. 220–240; Appendix 2: Alex Prossoff's story, pp. 242–248; Appendix 3: Personal history of war prisoners from Attu, pp. 249–254.

Prossoff, Alex
1988   Life Story. In *Journal of an Aleutian Year*. Ethel Ross Oliver. Seattle: University of Washington Press. Pp. 242248.

Scammon, C. M.
1874   *The Marine Mammals of the Northwestern Coast of North America*. Republished in 1968 with new introduction by V. B. Scheffer. New York: Dover Publications.

Shapsnikoff, Anfesia T., and Raymond L. Hudson
1974   *Aleut Basketry*. Anthropological Papers of the University of Alaska 16.

Spaulding, Albert C.
1962   *Archeological Investigations on Agattu, Aleutian Islands*. Anthropological Papers, Museum of Anthropology, University of Michigan 18:1–79.

Stein, Gary C.
n.d.   Uprooted: Native Casualties of the Aleutian Campaign of World War II. Manuscript. University of Alaska Fairbanks.

Stewart, Henry

1978   Preliminary Report Concerning the 1942 Japanese Invasion and Occupation of Attu and the Subsequent Removal of Attuans to Japan, 1942–1945. Report prepared for the Aleut/Pribilof Islands Association, Inc.

2008   Aleuts in Japan, 1942–1945. In *Alaska at War, 1941–1945: The Forgotten War Remembered*. Fern Chandonnet, ed. Fairbanks: University of Alaska Press. Pp. 301–304.

Sugiyama, Masami

1984   *Meetings Between Aleutian and Japanese People*. Tokyo: Sugiyama Publishing. Summarized and translated from Japanese by Hiroko Harada, 2010.

Unalaska City School

1981   *The Aleutian Invasion*. Unalaska, AK: Unalaska City School District.

US Census Office

1884   *Report on the Population, Industries, and Resources of Alaska*. 10th Census: 1880. [Ivan Petroff]. Washington: US Government Printing Office.

1940   US Census, Third Judicial District, Aleutian Islands.

US Coast Guard

1930   Records of the Bering Sea Patrol. 605-65, Box 17, NC-31, Entry 292, ARC 873. File 611.

1931   Records of the Bering Sea Patrol. 605-65, Box 17, NC-31, Entry 292, ARC 873. File: Report of Operations.

1939   Records of the Bering Sea Patrol. 810-141, Box 58, NC-31, Entry 292, ARC 873. Folder 611-601 (1939) Annual Reports.

West, Phoebe

1938   An Educational Program for an Aleut Village. Unpublished M.S. thesis, University of Washington.

Wright, Parascovia

1988   Interview notes, Debra Corbett. September 17.